A
FRENCH
AFFAIR

by the same author

Fiction

May You Die in Ireland
The Whole Hog
Green Grass
Out of Season
The 100,000 Welcomes
The Shooting of Dan McGrew
A Sorry State
Mr Big
Brainbox and Bull
The Rapist
Deep Pocket
The Elgar Variations
Zigzag
God Squad Bod
A Free-Range Wife
A Healthy Way to Die
Peckover Holds the Baby
Kill the Butler
Peckover Joins the Choir

A FRENCH AFFAIR

Michael Kenyon

St. Martin's Press
New York

Library of Congress Cataloging-in-Publication Data

Kenyon, Michael.
A French affair / Michael Kenyon.
p.   cm.
"A Thomas Dunne book."
ISBN 0-312-09295-4
1. Kenyon, Michael—Homes and haunts—France—Lot.   2. Novelists,
English—20th century—Biography.   3. Lot (France)—Social life and
customs.   4. British—France—Lot—Biography.   I. Title.
PR6061.E675Z466   1993
823'.914—dc20   93-696   CIP

First published in Great Britain by André Deutsch Limited.

First U.S. Edition: June 1993
10 9 8 7 6 5 4 3 2 1

For Cath, Lucy, Kate, and Polly

Acknowledgment

Some of these memories first appeared in *Gourmet*,
New York. The author thanks the magazine for
permission to adapt them for this book.

Contents

A
FRENCH
AFFAIR

Prologue

'ROLL ON, thou deep and dark blue ocean, roll!' I silently proclaimed in the prow of the ship, leaving my native land for ever.

Actually I was leaving for two weeks. This wasn't Byron's Aegean either, it was the English Channel, which is the colour of porridge, and the ship was the Calais-Dover ferry, reeking of engine oil and chips. The proclaiming was silent because also in the prow milled mobs of insentient British riffraff, my fellow countrymen, who, though embarrassing, were not deaf. Nothing was to be won by being led away for questioning and sedatives.

Calais was suddenly, unbelievably, abroad! The marvel was that the ground underfoot did not tilt, or talk back, or in some way behave foreignly, but was solid, as in England. Buildings, traffic, people, all were French. Through the windows of the train the fields were French, and the cars were fast black Citroëns from Jean Gabin gangster films or slow grey deux-chevaux from bucolic Fernandel films.

This was my first trip abroad: August, 1949, age eighteen. I was on an exchange, visiting a French boy, Guy, a serious, frowning lad who lived fifteen storeys up in a tower block with no lift at Porte d'Orléans on the southern perimeter of Paris. We didn't dislike each other, we simply had nothing to say, having only school French and school English and the effort of meeting half way being too great. After he had shown me the Eiffel Tower, Champs-Elysées, Sacré-Coeur, and Napoleon's tomb, I went my own way, which suited us both. Guy's parents came to accept that their visitor with the fixed romantic stare liked his solitude and could cope, more or less.

Going my own way meant taking the métro to the Left Bank or to Montmartre and walking endlessly. The purpose was to breathe Paris and pass as a Parisian, one who though currently misunderstood would one day show the world. As long as I kept my mouth shut and spoke to no one all day I probably did pass. On the other hand, people did not nudge each other and say, 'Zut, there goes a bohemian Parisian!'

The smells were of Gauloises, garlic (not that I knew then that it was garlic), roasting coffee, and drains. In those days every rue and boulevard accommodated us men with a cylindrical pissoir, or more politely, vespasienne, named after the Emperor Vespasian, who reputedly introduced public lavatories into Rome, then taxed them. Vespasian had a ribald wit, according to Suetonius, and he built the Colosseum, so it could be true. He didn't tax the lavatories themselves, he taxed the collection of urine, used as a source of ammonia in making cloth. Let's move on.

The store windows that riveted me were those crowded with wines and spirits. Byrrh, Dubonnet, Cognac, Cointreau, Pernod – what did it all mean? My previous experience with alcohol had been a sherry at Christmas.

On the Left Bank's Boul' Mich' (as we locals called it) I would be a Sorbonne student heading to Les Deux Magots for a word on existentialism with Sartre, Simone de Beauvoir, and fellow starving students. With Colette, too, and Sydney Bechet, when my imagination got really out of hand.

Montmartre was trickier, being peopled by pimps, tarts, and tourists, none of whom I cared to be identified with. I suppose I might have been an undercover cop reporting to Inspector Maigret, but cops were insensitive and unromantic, and anyway I had never heard of Inspector Maigret. I had heard only of Byron, Keats, and Shelley.

Thirsty for lowlife, I hauled out money when stopped in the Place Pigalle by a character peddling pornographic postcards, only one of which he permitted me to see before I paid. The exposed postcard was of a bare lady with a swan, which even in my heated condition I could not find that exciting. The others would be better. What I paid I don't recall but probably the budget for the day. The pedlar melted away. The postcards were of sculptures and paintings in the Louvre.

Back at Porte d'Orléans the evening meal was superior to what I was accustomed to: small portions but many courses, and slow. Melon, cold ham and sausage, hot fish with sauce, meat *au jus*, an unheard-of object named an artichoke, unknown endives, glazed peach tarts, bread with everything – and wine! Usually the wine was a red ordinaire to which we added water. However, more than once at dessert time Guy's father, an officer in the French army, uncorked a bottle of Cérons, a sweet white Bordeaux. Instead of the fifteen minutes I grew up with, these meals might last two hours.

Not breakfast, of course, which was a disaster. No bacon, eggs, toast, marmalade, and tea, but biscottes you either put apricot jam on or dunked in milky coffee. Biscottes were what in England we call rusks and give to teething babies. Once he has his teeth, no Brit eats this numbingly dull item again, until he comes to France where for breakfast it might be that or nothing.

More fun than Guy were his older brothers, Georges and André. They brought with them an element of risk. They spoke no English but they laughed and winked a good deal and took me to the Folies Bergères. If it wasn't the Folies Bergères, it was the Casino de Paris. Memory falters. It wasn't the Moulin Rouge, where Toulouse-Lautrec sketched cancan girls, because the Moulin Rouge no longer existed, and where we went was a respectable theatre, more's the pity, with no dancing except from the chorus line on stage. At the Folies Bergères (or Casino de Paris) was a cast of a thousand bare breasts and bottoms, which in all conscience was thrilling, far back in the theatre though we were.

3

I was fresh from nine years at boys' boarding schools, and these were the first ladies' breasts and bottoms I had seen outside *National Geographic* and the airbrushed naturist magazine, *Health and Efficiency*. The show included glittering costumes, a gross comedian with a banana named Dando, horses and jugglers, all of little consequence. The bare ladies were it. Oh gosh, oh golly!

And yet. This was so patently show business, not authentic lowlife, that in the end it disappointed. No genuine, self-respecting bohemian would have sat in that audience at the Folies Bergères. Had I known that most of the bottoms were not even French, but British, Swedish, Dutch even, I'd have felt even more let down.

For moral and spiritual cleansing I was encouraged to leave the fleshpots of Paris and visit Guy's grandmother, Mémé, and his aunt and uncle at L'Escale, their bar-restaurant in Meulan, a small town on the Seine twenty miles away.

At L'Escale I would eat like a king, enthused Guy's parents, unaware that la bonne table was not high among my priorities. Had I tried to explain that food was unpoetic and lacked soul, they would have been bewildered. Guy was offered as company because Mémé, aunt, and uncle, though welcoming, would be too busy to entertain me, except on Monday, the day the restaurant closed, when they would be too tired. I must have managed to convey that, delightful as Guy's companionship would be, I would be fine, he mustn't drag himself away. That was one of the rare times I knew Guy to smile.

Meulan, north-west of Paris, is not to be confused with Melun, to the south-east. Melun has a population of many thousands, a philosophy school founded in 1101 by Abelard, and eel pie as a speciality. Meulan had nothing so fabulous, being more a village than a town, though switching from comatose weekdays to animated weekends, when Parisians swarmed in to inhale, walk in the woods, fish in the Seine, and eat at L'Escale. France has countless such restaurants:

4

dependable, unpretentious, smelling of cooking and floor soap. Inside they are dark until your eyes adjust. Outside, in summer, the sun dazzles. An escale is a port of call. Many riverside restaurants are named L'Escale.

Roger, the uncle, when not serving in the bar, kept himself in shape by exercising with dumbbells. This he did indoors, wearing his barman's black trousers and an undervest. He had spindly legs, biceps like cannonballs, and white Alps of shoulders and chest. No worship of the god of suntan for Roger. Sun was for ripening the tomatoes and string beans in the garden.

Paulette, the aunt, was forever telling me that illusions were for youth and I should cling to them. This wisdom seemed to hold a flaw but I couldn't quite put my finger on it. Now that I look back I suspect Paulette would have liked illusions of her own to cling to but had none. What I'd said to cause her to go on about illusions I don't know, but I hear her still. 'Gardez vos illusions, Michel.'

She was a lively peroxide blonde with whom I must have been more than a little in love. Clearly she understood about dreams and illusions. She never ceased sweeping, scrubbing, washing dishes, hanging out laundry, and waiting on table. She was the first woman I encountered, outside the silver screen, whose lipstick did not follow the contours of her lips but built a cupid's bow where none existed. In a French film, she, the older woman, would have introduced me, the melancholy nincompoop, to sexual passion, as Micheline Presle did for Gérard Philipe in *Le Diable au Corps*.

Mémé, the grandmother, was large, gruff, bristly, and the boss. No nonsense about dreams and illusions here. Mémé must have been eighty. She did all the cooking, ate with the appetite of a wrestler, and every morning at six o'clock collected her baskets and caught the train to Paris. At Les Halles she would buy everything needed for the day's menus, then return laden to L'Escale. She bought nothing for the next day.

Meals with the family were at erratic hours. Lunch was often at three o'clock, after the last customers had gone,

5

and closer to four on Sunday. Not that bohemians minded waiting, or even going without. Where I erred was in failing to ask not when but what.

Mémé, Roger, and Paulette knew the menu and therefore how to pace themselves. I didn't, and believed it ungentlemanly to inquire. To ask would have been to betray curiosity, thereby hinting at greed, apprehension, or both. Anyway, what if I had asked? Morue, they would have said, tucking their napkins in at the neck. Or cabillaud. Or cervelles de veau. All meaningless. How many and how much was what I needed to know.

Breakfast was a lifetime ago, if breakfast was the word for that bleak non-event, here as at Porte d'Orléans. At lunch, listing from hunger, I would assault the heaped platter of starters. Forget Bohemia. Here was quartered melon, ham, radishes, butter, country bread, sweet, misshapen tomatoes sliced in a vinaigrette, circles of cooked red sausage embedded with gobbets of blinding-white fat, and fantastic khaki-coloured mush which was pâté of something. When the next course arrived I was a bent reed, if not yet totally broken. While Mémé, Roger, and Paulette ploughed into their poached salmon with sorrel sauce I had to force myself. When next came chicken or steak with french fries, peas, sauce, and more bread, I could only twitch.

Unless you asked what the meal was to be, nothing could be taken for granted. A course, even two courses, might be missing, the customers having been more numerous than anticipated. Once we started with lobster. This was my first lobster. I had difficulty getting at the flesh, and when I found it was not sure I cared for it. Lobster didn't hold a candle to pâté, of which not a sign. Mémé, Paulette, and Roger, aromatic from a burst with the dumbbells, probed and dug expertly, crunching on claws, fingers dripping mayonnaise, mouths and chins glistening. Preferring for once to save myself for the slabs of lamb or whatever was to come, I offered my hearty leftovers. Without inquiring into my motives, they accepted.

6

But that was it. Lobster. Nothing was to come, only boring cheese and grapes. My hosts repaired to their posts in the kitchen, bar, and at the ironing board. I returned to the river. The garden at L'Escale sloped down to the hot, untenanted Seine where every day for five days I rowed for hours, armed with Byron, bothered only by mosquitoes, brooding in moody ecstacy on girls and mortality, and either bloated with food or starving.

Back in Paris I bought a present to take home to my parents: green Chartreuse, or it may have been Crème de Menthe. I remember only that the choice was based on the vivid green colour. The gift was accepted with pleasure and placed beside the sherry in the dining-room cupboard, where it lasted several years.

1 A Little About the Lot

A FARMER in a beret bounces along the lane in his Citroën deux-chevaux and halts outside our rented holiday house. He is either a farmer or a hijacker of farm produce. He opens the back of the car to reveal tray upon tray of cantaloupe melons and nectarines at laughably low prices. 'Over-production,' he says. Clearly if people don't help him out he will be having to eat all the melons and nectarines himself. We buy a tray of each and lunch beside the swimming pool on melon, pâté, knobby, scarred tomatoes which actually taste of tomato, red wine, a loaf of bread, goat's cheese, and nectarines. In the Lot valley in August the sun shines through sybaritic days.

We are twenty-five years on from the days of Byron and Guy. (Guy, are you well? How did we come to lose touch so fast?) Not that I was to know it but that first sortie across the Channel marked the start of a lifelong love affair with France. True, an on-off affair, neglect alternating with rediscovery, delight with vexation. Now, in the mid-seventies, a paterfamilias, bourgeois and unashamed, I am here with my family to live.

It will be all right, won't it? We'll manage? We have to manage because there is no going back to London, not for the next twelve months. We have let our house to the Venezuelan vice-consul (at least that's who he says he is), and he has moved in with many Venezuelan relatives. We found the cat a cozy home a few doors along on the terraced street, loaded the car until it squeaked, and took the ferry to Dieppe, that being the handiest port for France's south-west.

We have been to this hot, bosky spot two or three times before, once for the best part of a year. The girls were very small then and the village school suited them well enough, except when they had their hair pulled and knuckles struck by the teacher, a routine procedure in France for which there is no redress. Now that they're bigger they may escape bodily harm. We shall find out.

These last August days of gross, nectarine-eating hedonism are not going to last, fortunately. For some of us northern Europeans, imbued with guilt and the work ethic, sunshine and idleness pall quickly enough. In excess they bring on anxiety attacks. Tomorrow the dozen miles to the big city, Cahors, capital of the Lot and of this ancient province of Quercy, and the business of arranging our future as residents of France. We must search for a furnished flat. Schools have to be found. Catherine, my wife, hopes to find a job. What jobs will there be for a London schoolteacher in this depopulated *département* of the Lot?

No job problem for Monsieur. Writers have two advantages. We can wear whatever we like and live anywhere.

Where is the Lot and why here? If a writer can live anywhere, and can talk his family into it, why not Bali? Why not the Scottish Highlands? Tuscany? San Francisco? If the country is to be France – France giving this husband and wife an agreeable glow – why not a region we have heard of? Provence, on a herb-perfumed hilltop a hop and a skip from the soupy Mediterranean. Or Brittany with its oysters and dolmens. Were I to do it again I might plump for Burgundy. All that rolling greenness, mustard, and unaffordable wine. France's problem is too much choice.

Drive from one of the Channel ports to Spain and you'll probably pass through Cahors. We are 600 kilometres from

Paris – 375 miles – and another 200 miles from the Pyrenees. Just to the north is the Dordogne, which began filling up with British, Dutch and Parisian holiday home owners in the late fifties and sixties. When the price of a vacation house in the Dordogne soared out of sight, and no more were left anyway, unless you settled for a pile of rubble and rotting timbers, the invasion pressed south. By the eighties the Lot was filling up. Still they come, in the nineties, though the pickings, I gather, are slim.

The French pronounce the t in the Lot. The h and s in Cahors are silent. Ka-or, the Ka with an a as in a Yorkshireman's bath, grass, mask. Anyway, not Kay-horse.

The Lot, a bureaucrat's handiwork, is in the old province of Quercy, on the western edge of the Massif Central. Quercy, Dordogne, Périgord, Guyenne, Gascony, these are all provinces of the former kingdom of Aquitaine. But Quercy is a word frequently met in the Lot. The cuisine, the fatted, truffled goose liver, and the fatty, preserved duck, is Quercinoise. The walnuts and the prune liqueur are of Quercy and labelled as such.

The river Lot spills into the Garonne, which empties into the Atlantic at Bordeaux. Away from the river Lot's fertile valley – fruit, maize, tobacco – the limestone hills are arid, stony, and matted with juniper and scrofulous oak trees. *Quercus* is the Latin for oak. These hills are good for nothing except vines and walking off the goose liver. In cleared areas may stand a hut built stone by stone by shepherds for shelter against vile weather. This is cave country. You stand in line, pay your admission, and follow subterraneously a student earning holiday money by explaining it all in French. Remember, stalaCtites point down from the Ceiling, stalaGmites sprout up from the Ground. On the walls are prehistoric paintings of mammoth and deer. Astonishing! How did these people, our ancestors, dare venture into these black pits, and then, of all things, paint pictures on the walls? The Gouffre du Padirac has no paintings but is 325 feet deep. You tour it by boat. Take woollies, it's freezing down there.

Compton Mackenzie introduced us to the area. One evening in the late sixties we turned on BBC TV and there he was being interviewed, venerable and twinkling. Having missed most of the programme we had no idea where he was, but it was somewhere in France and looked idyllic. He sat in a garden under hanging vines, not displeased with himself. He had lived in a multitude of places in quest of the perfect spot, especially islands – the Channel Islands, the Hebrides, Capri. Catherine said we must write to him and ask where this place was.

Sir Compton was a prolific middlebrow novelist. As a lad I was knocked out by his *Sinister Street*, a passionate and, to my mind, slightly risqué story of a brother and sister growing up. His *Whisky Galore* became one of the first Ealing comedies (*Tight Little Island* in America). Fay Compton, his sister, was a West End actress whom I used to muddle with Sybil Thorndyke. I was eleven or twelve at the time, an age when grown-ups are easy to muddle.

I wrote to Compton Mackenzie care of his publisher. He wrote back saying the place was Cazals, in the Lot. Scouring the houses-to-let (France) columns, we failed to find a mention of Cazals, but in Catus, twenty miles away, was a four-bedroom, two-bathroom renovated farmhouse.

The owner was a gentleman farmer in Cambridgeshire who descended on his hideaway for a month in the summer and was happy to let it when he was at home in England farming. After our first summer holiday there we asked if we might rent it for the autumn and winter too. This troubled him. His custom was to turn off the water and close the place down for the winter. Nobody had lived there in winter, not since he had bought it and done it up. Winter, he understood, could be chilly in the Lot. Letters passed back and forth. His letters were agitated. He clearly wished we hadn't asked. He said there was a fireplace in the living room but we would need back-up gas heaters. We knew there was a fireplace in the living room, a vast area with a tiled, chequerboard floor and a stone sink without taps or water. We said we would get a gas heater. He said all right then, deeply perturbed. He knew the Lot better than we did.

That winter was exceptionally cold and snowy. Wherever you find yourself in this world, chances are that the locals will tell you the weather happens to be exceptional just now, it's not usually like this. Snow fell from December to April. We'd have been better off in the Alps, the girls could at least have learned to ski. Getting up in the morning, dressing, we jostled for position beside our roaring gas heater, five of us. Lucy got closest because she was older and bigger than her sisters, and her parents couldn't toss her aside to make room for themselves. Lucy got so close she set herself on fire. First came an acrid smell. The next moment flames were licking up her legs. Squeals, whomping of flames, stripping off of chic, combustible nightie and stamping thereon, as in a voodoo rite. Lucy was packed off to school anyway. (The crafty ruses of children for a day off school are beyond belief.)

The next night I awoke from dreams of shooting the rapids and lay awake listening to a pandemonium of crickets outside. Crickets in January? If it wasn't crickets, what was it, this unceasing susurration?

Water was pouring through the living room ceiling, stood a foot deep on the tiled chequerboard floor, and was rising. Either the roof had fallen in or a pipe had burst. If the latter, I couldn't see myself doing much about it, not being a plumber.

A burst pipe it was, gushing water in an untenanted room filled with dead moths under the roof. Coping wasn't difficult after I had given up trying to staunch the flood with my thumb. I turned every tap I could find on the maze of pipes whichever way it would turn. The gushing stopped.

The girls had to be roused. We opened the living room door to the terrace, so letting some of the floodwater out and the snow in. We bailed out with saucepans and swept out with brooms. Disposing of a lake of frigid water at three in the morning in pyjamas is a chore one wouldn't want to make a habit of.

Having no telephone, and France's telephone system at that epoch being idiosyncratic anyway, especially for a foreigner with inadequate French, I wrote to our landlord, cozy in Cambridgeshire, regaling him with the incident. The letter was lighthearted, breezy. No lives had been lost. Winter in the Lot was magnifique. The sparkle of the snow. He wrote back to say we should have shut off the water when the weather grew cold. His letter was unamused, even testy. He gave us the name of his plumber in Catus. Not a word of praise for my prowess in quenching the flood.

So tomorrow the big city. For the present the only problem is enjoying these melons and nectarines before the wasps move in, though we are probably too late. The advance wasp guard is here, scouting. Soon they will be joined by their sisters and their cousins (whom we reckon up by dozens) and their aunts. French wasps are infinitely more tiresome than British wasps. Here they have fresher, more aromatic melons to alight on. We've tried swatting them, flailing the air with a newspaper, which of course drives them crazy, and we've tried ignoring them, which takes some doing when one of the brutes stalks along the back of your hand, across the knuckles, then pauses on a finger, waiting, testing your courage. Capturing the wasps in a jammy apricot jam jar worked not badly until the girls decided they could not bear to see the wasps trapped and struggling. An English painter friend who owns a summer home near Fumel, further along the valley, was amazed we didn't light joss sticks. Never failed, he said. We lit joss sticks on our alfresco table and watched the wasps home in, inhaling and frolicking. A shopkeeper in the village told us with relish of a recent newspaper item about a man killed by a wasp which fell into his glass of wine. Unaware, the man swallowed a mouthful of wine plus the wasp, which stung him mortally in his inside. We comfort ourselves that he probably had an allergy. But how are you to know you have an allergy until it's too late?

The sun pours down. Lucy, aged thirteen, has swum two lengths of the pool under water without a breath. Moreover, we have company. The youngest boy from the farm along the lane has arrived on his bicycle to swim and play rummy with Kate, nine, and Polly, eight. His bicycle has ten speeds. Our bicycles in London have one speed (slow) and a shopping basket on the handlebar. The French are bicycle fanatics who all summer long are to be seen strung out along the highways, between fields of sunflowers, wearing coloured jerseys and crash helmets, and pedalling like the wind. Patrick Becquet, from the farm, is well-mannered, handsome, and short, even for a twelve-year-old, though perhaps not for a French twelve-year-old. Somewhere I heard that the French and the Latins of the Mediterranean generally tend to be short because of their constant fighting with each other down the ages. The young and fit would go off to the wars; the less sturdy stayed behind and became the progenitors. Maybe yes, maybe no.

What, we ask Patrick, had he had for lunch? None of our business but we like to know. No sense coming to live in France and not being maniacal about food. Soup, he says. The soup of the region is a thin, bland vegetable soup fortified with noodles or stale bread. Then, he says, string beans (cold) with a dressing, pizza, rabbit in a sauce (unspecified), cheese, flan, and naturally bread and wine. The pizza is a surprise. This is the first we've heard of anyone hereabouts eating pizza. Had his father drunk *le chabrot*? Patrick shyly supposes he had. *Le chabrot* is the rustic habit of adding a trickle of wine to any remnants in the soup plate, swirling the mixture, then lifting the plate with both hands to the mouth and drinking. The urban middle classes consider the custom quaint but vulgar.

The Becquets' stone farmhouse is close on four hundred years old. Carved in the mighty chimney breast in the kitchen is the date 1619. The family has a score of sheep, four cows, two pigs, and squadrons of free-ranging poultry. They are virtually self-supporting, growing all their own vegetables, and with grapes enough to keep them in wine. They have walnut, plum, and apple trees. They sell their milk, some of their walnuts, all their harvest of corn, and in a good

15

year several profitable kilos of truffles nosed out by Diane, their truffle dog. From the geese Madame Becquet produces lucrative foie gras. Their life seems hard though, and they've told us that this summer of drought has been a disaster. Nothing has succeeded except the grapes, and if bad weather should arrive before the harvest at the end of September, they too will fail.

When did farmers not grumble? Are the Becquets headed for the poorhouse or are they comfortable? Monsieur Becquet, a fine-looking, hospitable man, was born in the farmhouse, as were his father and grandfather. Two years ago builders fitted the house with its first bathroom, and this year a telephone has been installed. Their kitchen – the French rarely show visitors beyond the kitchen and living room – has an electric stove, dishwasher, refrigerator, and television. A sceptical schoolmaster in the village tells us that the farmers of the Lot are better off than they pretend. They receive fat subsidies and are magicians with tax returns. When the rest of us have gone under from famine, flood, and lightning bolt, farmers such as the Becquets will be sitting down at their kitchen table and tucking in their napkins.

They will not be sitting down to truffles every day, but here, and more famously in the neighbouring Périgord, is truffle country. Also killer foie gras at a million calories a mouthful (except that research in the nineties will question whether foie gras is a killer, but more of that anon). Confits of goose and duck, cooked in their own fat and preserved in airtight jars, pile on more calories, but who's counting. The recipe for longevity – hereabouts there are plenty of people in their eighties and nineties – is adequate bread and salad with the foie gras and confit, and as well as wine, lots of mineral water.

Still, if you need your cholesterol topping up, this is the place. Here, too, are cèpes, which are slimy wild mushrooms sometimes approaching beachball size. Damp, sumptuous walnut cakes. Plump and fleshy prunes soaked in brandy or stuffed with marzipan paste or with a purée of more prunes or with Lord knows what. Whatever someone has done to them they are a different beast from the watery, disintegrating school prunes in wartime Yorkshire that were supposed to keep us regular. The deep red, almost black Cahors wine was a favourite of Peter the Great of Russia, he who banished his first wife to a convent and had twelve children by his second. With the wine a couple of knockout native cheeses: Cabécou, a circular goat cheese two inches across, its texture varying from crumbly to liquid, and Cantal, a hard cheese not unlike a good Cheddar, and mild, medium, or strong, depending on how much you are willing to pay. Actually, Cantal is not native to the Lot but to Cantal, the next *département* to the north-east, in the Auvergne, but I would guess more Cantal is eaten in the Lot than any other single cheese, including Camembert. For pushing the boat out the Lotois go for Roquefort. Perhaps the French everywhere do. Roquefort does not come from the Lot either but from Roquefort, eighty or ninety miles south-east of Cahors.

South from the Lot to Toulouse, Castelnaudry, and Carcassonne, is cassoulet, the bean stew with preserved goose and mutton which takes days to make. Anatole France, man of letters, adored the cassoulet of a Madame Clémence who never made anything else, presumably because she hadn't the time. 'To be good it must have cooked very slowly for a long time,' he wrote. 'Clémence's cassoulet had been cooking for twenty years.'

Advice to visitors: Stay clear of debate about cassoulet. Depending on where you are, each cassoulet is different and each infinitely superior to all others. Offer, in Castelnaudry, the view that cassoulet should include partridge and sausage, as did the cassoulet you were served last week in Toulouse, and you will be thought out of your mind. Especially do not sound off about cassoulet à la minute which is made in one hour (canned white kidney beans for a start) by chef and cookbook writer Pierre Franey, a Burgundian transplanted to New York. You will be shrugged off as invincibly ignorant, possibly patted and comforted, and asked, 'What does anyone from Burgundy know of cassoulet?'

17

To every region of France its epicurean glories, but three regions above all, we've heard it said, are more gloriously epicurean than the rest: Burgundy (impertinences with cassoulet notwithstanding), Normandy, and here in the south-west.

We have presented Monsieur Becquet with his bottle of Scotch, a gift he has come to expect. Some years ago when we gave him his first bottle he didn't much care for it, he tells us now. He was too polite to say anything. But he persevered and now has a taste for it.

He has given us the ritual bottle of eau-de-vie de marc, though we are far from acquiring a taste for this ferocious distillate of the dregs of the wine pressings. Catherine will render it palatable by adding fruit, thereby transforming an inherently evil potion into ratafia, a fruit liqueur. Marc is becoming increasingly rare. Farmers are allowed to distil it only under licence. Inspectors drop in, pry, and measure quantities and alcohol content. No inheriting or passing on of the licence either. The licence expires with the death of the holder. The government is attempting to phase out inebriation by marc which seems destined to become a bootleg hooch, equivalent to poteen in County Kerry and moonshine in Tennessee.

This year's bottle from M Becquet is not colourless but pale brown and has a wooden ladder in it. The brown colour, M Becquet explains, comes from the ladder. Sailors put ships into bottles, M Becquet puts in a ladder.

Friends in London reacted to our immigration with either 'Goodness, you're lucky!' or 'Gracious, you're brave!' Time will tell. Will the language be a delight or an insurmountable block?

Lucy has good French, thanks to her year at the Catus village school. Kate and Polly attended too, but they were infants. Whatever French they may have learned there they have forgotten, apart from one drummed-in poem they will remember all their lives. Me too. The beginning of it anyway.

> J'ai rencontré trois escargots
> Qui s'en allaient, cartable à dos.

Translation: I met three snails going along with satchels on their backs. After the snails the poet meets three slugs, and so on with various beasts through many couplets.

Shortly, Kate and Polly will be dropped in at the deep end of some big, free school in Cahors where much good those trois escargots will do them. Their parents strive not to betray anxiety. It won't last long, will it, the incomprehension, the utter at-seaness amid multitudes of ruffians, their classmates, talking only French and probably coarse street French at that?

My French is slightly superior to my wife's. So far. But she loves the language, is resolved to become proficient, and will soon outstrip me. She has asked to sit in on classes at the village school, simply to be in the thick of French, and has been welcomed. Highly unlikely that a stray foreigner in London would be allowed to sit in on school lessons. Before coming here we invested in a course of teach-yourself-French, put record number one on the gramophone, and hunched over the text, mouthing along with the the instructor's impeccable articulation. But oh, those French Rs! Try saying, French-style, Rue de Rivoli.

Lucy is diving for centimes. Patrick, Kate and Polly have departed up the lane with colanders to pick blackberries for a crumble. That's a laugh. They will return with no more blackberries than will fill an eggcup, but with full bellies and empurpled fingers and mouths. Cath is looking up a word in *Le Petit Larousse*, the illustrated dictionary found in most French homes.

Why not another glass of red? Thanks very much. First checking for wasps, of course.

2 Metropolis

'MONSIEUR, WE'RE looking for a furnished flat for one year in the centre of Cahors, preferably the old quarter – la vielle ville, oui?'

The first agent sighs and shakes his head. The second has a hard time controlling his mirth. He has heard nothing so rich all summer. A third believes she will have something in the New Year, but it's a house in the country, seventeen miles away. A fourth hustles rubbish. From his sales pitch, his weasel eyes, and our experience in helping to track down holiday places for friends, we know what he's trying to unload: gimcrack rooms at millionaire prices for high-season tourists.

Cahors is not that big a city. Population 22,000. Today the town is celebrated for the Pont Valentré, a fortified medieval bridge over the river Lot, still very much in use. We like it here – the narrow streets of the old quarter, the smells of roasting coffee and frying garlic, the sight of black-shawled peasant women bringing live chickens and rabbits to market, the measured pace of life, the calm – but already we have run out of agents and have nowhere to live. If Cahors has no place for us we shall have to move on. We can't go back to London and we're not spending another winter at the Catus house, driving the girls along twelve miles of twisting road to school at eight every morning and gathering them up at five to bring them back. Not that the Cambridgeshire landlord would want us for another winter.

Moving on might not be so bad. The vagabond life. Our geography would improve. It's not as if we have close friends in Cahors. We know only three or four people. In Catus we know the husband and wife schoolteachers, the pharmacist and his family, and the Becquets. We have several English friends with summer houses but they're all an hour's drive away. Either Bordeaux (population 226,000) or Toulouse (383,000) would offer more scope than pokey Cahors.

'No harm in just looking at that unfurnished place,' says Catherine, who from time to time is deserted by all sense of reality. This flat is slap in the middle of town, the rent is reasonable, but it's unfurnished. We possess not a chair, not a blanket, not even a knife, fork, or cup.

The flat is on the second floor over a glittering ironmongery in the rue Joffre, a sloping one-way street leading from the main boulevard to the market square and the cathedral. Also on the street are a cobbler, furrier, bookshop, tobacconist, wool shop with wicker baskets of wool on the pavement (French women are enthusiastic knitters – remember those films about the French Revolution where the women look up from their knitting only to watch the guillotine lop off another head?), sports shop with gundog snoozing on the step, and sundry gloomy doors behind which lies we know not what. We climb the steps above the ironmongery. The young woman from the agency lets us in with a gaoler's key.

When as potential tenants we look at an apartment I never look at the apartment. I watch Catherine. Watching now as we step into a bare, lofty kitchen with a sink like a Roman bath, a coal stove, and a view across a courtyard to the mellow brick of the town hall, I suspect trouble ahead. We tour spacious rooms with dust-laden radiators and shuttered windows reaching from floor to ceiling. Space and emptiness. Catherine is enchanted. She throws open shutters and murmurs, 'It's like *Last Tango in Paris*,' adding cryptically, 'without Marlon Brando.'

So this is to be it. The girls are racing about deciding who will have which room. We have still a few days in which to corner the scattered English colony and scrounge before they lock up their summer homes and head north. Our few French friends rally too, discovering in cellars and attics cobwebbed furniture, old army blankets, and cartons of crockery, which they never knew they had. We borrow, forage, loot.

Our week as furniture removers is for the most part erased from memory by that defence mechanism in the brain that blots out life's more trying experiences. Dimly I recall a ton of Victorian double bed too big for the stairs. The artist, a Fulham squash champion, who had recommended joss sticks as the answer for wasps, helped haul the bedstead by ropes up the outside of the building. The whole of the rue Joffre turned out to stare. From doorways emerged shopkeepers and customers, watching wide-eyed for signs of slipping knots and ensuing calamity. The British are too polite and inhibited to notice anything so embarrassing as a bed as big as a boat being lifted up the side of a building. Not so the French. They assemble to advise, exhort, and do anything except mind their own business.

The only disaster of moving-in week befalls a borrowed *matelas*, a mattress, spanking new, of purest lamb's wool, loaned to us by the pharmacist in Catus. His brother, a career mattress-maker, had made it by hand. I load the *matelas* at our holiday farmhouse. Having tied the bed's base upside-down to our Renault's roofrack, I have no more string. I wedge the mattress securely into the base and set off with caution along the lane and onto the road to Cahors. It's a sunny Sunday morning, the opening day of la chasse, the hunting season. The hills are alive with the sound of gunfire. When I arrive half an hour later in the rue Joffre the mattress is gone.

I retrace the route, looking to left and right along the grassy verges, into ditches, up the centre of the road, and down hillsides. No *matelas*. It can hardly have blown away. A string of racing bicyclists might have collided with it, and the bloodied mattress with adhering bicycle spokes and skin been taken to the Police Judiciaire as evidence. At fifteen miles an hour I round a curve in the serpentine lane to the holiday house and drive into two armed hunters and a dog who burst from the woods in pursuit of a rabbit. I miss the rabbit and the hunters but hit the dog, bending its paw. The village vet, who is also the mayor, bandages the paw and assures us that in three weeks the dog will be hunting again.

When I report the loss of the *matelas* at Catus gendarmerie, the beefy policeman scowls and says, '*Matelot?*' By now my nerves are affecting my French. The policeman seems to suspect he may be being conned with a yarn about a sailor lost from a roofrack somewhere on the road to Cahors. When he grasps *matelas* he guffaws. He summons his mate from his typewriter. 'Monsieur, no one in this country hands in anything found on the road!' he cries. 'You should have had a label on it – Beware of Fleas!' Very droll. But in France, or no matter where, when a policeman laughs, you laugh.

We never found the mattress. 'Ce n'est pas grave,' says the pharmacist with an airy wave of his hand. He does not waive a cash reimbursement, however, and in his place I wouldn't have either. A pity the mattress had to be lamb's wool, not wood shavings and old turnip tops.

But we're here, furnished, in the rue Joffre. I like the name rue Joffre. Was it not Marshal Joffre in World War One who said either 'They shall not pass' or 'My centre is giving way, my right is in retreat, situation excellent. I shall attack'? No, it wasn't. The first, I discover, was Marshal Pétain, the second Marshal Foch. Joffre never said anything. My *Cambridge Biographical Dictionary* describes him as 'silent, patient, mathematical'. Rue Foch is the next street to ours and has a fancy grocery like a mini-Fortnum and Mason. That grocery will be our only resource if ever we need anything truly exotic, like Christmas pudding or Bovril.

If anything we are overfurnished, apart from one lamb's wool mattress. We have armchairs, chests of drawers, a fridge, even a carpet. We also have our first visitor, Monsieur Vallon, a scowling retired gentleman from a neighbouring flat.

He comes with a complaint, something to do with letter boxes. 'J'étais tellement étonné,' he says, standing to attention in the kitchen. 'Monsieur, Madame, j'étais tellement étonné.'

So he was astonished, why does he have to keep saying it? On the stone wall inside the entrance to the building are a half dozen tin letter boxes with a keyhole and a slot for a card with the owner's name. Four boxes were active. I had commandeered the remaining two with the intention of asking the postman which he recommended and did it matter? One had no lock, the other had a bent door and an apple core inside. 'J'étais tellement étonné,' M. Vallon says, one of the boxes evidently being his. So why doesn't he put his name on it? Catherine apologizes. I grovel – 'Mes regrets, Monsieur, excusez-moi' – and assure him the error will be rectified immediately. He says, 'J'étais tellement étonné.' Are we supposed to kill ourselves? It isn't as if anyone writes to him. I wouldn't. Is his box the one with no lock or the one with the apple core? He leaves, still scowling. We refuse to accept that this pipsqueak will be typical of life ahead. We are here, Cahors, France. How could we even have considered moving on?

Last year, 1975, President Valéry Giscard d'Estaing awarded the Legion of Honour to master chef Paul Bocuse as a reward for naming a truffle soup after him: *Soupe aux truffes* VGE. The French have their priorities right. When did a British cook receive a knighthood in the Honours List?

That same patrician president, visiting Cahors, and lauding the beauty and variety of France in general, singled out Cahors in particular as an ideal spot to live. Perhaps in Boulogne he singles out Boulogne. He's a politician. Nothing is more important than votes. But in praising the charm of Cahors he is on safe ground.

Tomorrow, schools.

La rentrée. The re-entry, the return to factory, office and school, the resumption of workaday life after the summer vacation. The word dominates shop windows and advertisements. On the radio it recurs every five minutes. The first leaves are falling, walnuts and chestnuts are beginning to drop, and la rentrée is the chief fact of life in Cahors and throughout France.

In Britain the holidays are spread out over several months. The country never closes down completely. In the United States most people have two weeks vacation, which is unbelievable, feudal, to the French, who take five weeks minimum, as do most British, Germans, and Scandinavians. In July the French crouch on their starting blocks for August. In August off they herd to beach and countryside. *August in Paris* could be an intriguing song. In Paris scarcely a Parisian remains other than hoteliers, waiters, and pick-pockets. The summer closedown being so profound in France, the September rentrée is abrupt and dramatic.

(Never, ever, put your car on the road in France during the last weekend in August. Everyone else in France – population 56 million – is on the road, returning home for the rentrée.)

For Lucy, Kate, and Polly, the rentrée is to new schools, new teachers. Inquiries having revealed that no school stands out above others, and none is to be avoided at all cost; we choose for convenience those closest to the rue Joffre. We present ourselves, sign forms, and that's that.

On the opening day of school at Groupe Sud Primary, a ten-minute walk away, Catherine and I join the mêlée in the playground: a bedlam of raised voices, milling children, scores of mothers, about four fathers, and teachers with clipboards calling out names and blowing whistles. Kate and Polly stand silent with new satchels and obligatory pinafores. The colour and design of the new satchel from Prisunic, the big chain store on the Boulevard Gambetta, dominates the start of their school year now and for years to come, even into adolescence when the fashion will shift from shiny and new to battered army bags with graffiti: *Vive les Stones!* and *J'aime Denis!* We watch crocodiles of children led away to classrooms. Finally only a few forlorn small fry and their parents remain, such as us. No more names are called.

Are the names Kate and Polly too difficult for the French to pronounce? We keep an eye on a distant underworld figure in a pearl grey suit and felt hat who clearly has clout. Adults have approached him and paid homage as if to a mafia godfather. He has surveyed the proceedings without ever blowing a whistle or becoming involved. He looks like George Raft in a Warner Brothers movie, circa 1940. He is the headmaster. We are never to see him without his hat, outdoors or in. He approaches, in tow a studious, bespectacled young man.

Kate and Polly, he tells us, are to be in a special class for six children from overseas, a language-oriented class with films, tapes, and the latest in audio-visual equipment. He beams with pride. This is the first time Groupe Sud has embarked on such a project. He introduces the studious young man as the teacher of the class, Monsieur Spiaggi.

Spiaggi? An Italian? We hearken closely to Monsieur Spiaggi's 'Bonjour' and detect an unmistakeable Neapolitan inflection.

None of this bodes well. We don't wish to seem ungrateful but a state-of-the-art, language-oriented class is not what we'd had in mind. When Lucy was tipped into her Catus village school with compulsory pinafore, slate, and chalk – it sounds like Dotheboys' Hall – she floundered but survived, made friends, and emerged fluent and, we like to think, unscarred. Are audio-visual machinery and classmates from beyond the Mediterranean a better idea? Presumably this clutch of uncomprehending children huddled with us in the yard are to be Kate and Polly's classmates. We bid our daughters farewell and walk back to the rue Joffre.

That evening the main concern of Kate and Polly is that tomorrow they take croissants and chocolate to school. During la récré – presumably recreation time, already they are learning gutter French but what would their Neapolitan teacher know? – everyone had had croissants and cake and biscuits and fruit and chocolate to eat. No future in trying to persuade Kate and Polly that everyone had not had bacon and egg for breakfast, they'd had a baby's rusk.

So what is their new teacher like and is he Italian? The girls don't know what he is. (He is in fact a one hundred

26

per cent Frenchman who may well never have set foot on Italian soil.) He's nice but he can't speak English, Kate says. He can't even count. What, we cry, not count at all? Not count in English, the girls say. They had plunged straight into film number one: 'Bonjour, Maman. Bonjour, Paul. Bonjour, Maman. Bonjour, Martine. Bonjour, Maman . . .' It sounds like our teach-yourself-French records. Their classmates, they say, are three Portuguese, or Spanish, and someone from Africa, like an Arab, or an Indian.

Term at Collège Gambetta starts the following day. We ask Lucy if she'd like us to walk there with her. On the whole she thinks not. As I must go to the post office, one block beyond the school, I compromise, setting out with her, then crossing the street and continuing independently.

Against the wall, awaiting the unlocking of the doors, straggles a disorderly mob of two or three hundred young teenagers, the youth of Cahors. These are the ones who, in times of political unrest, will take to the streets and tear up paving stones. Lucy, tall and blonde, strides in the direction of the doors to a symphony of whistles from the short, swarthy schoolboys. She marches on, head up, upper lip defiantly stiff, wobbling somewhat in her fashionable clogs. I press on along the other side of the street, uncertain whether to feel infuriated at the impudence of these hooligans or delighted that she is noticed. The French male evidently notices the female from an early age. When I look back the doors have opened and a blonde head is being sucked through like flotsam on a turbulent, dark flood.

School, we gather from Lucy that evening, had been all right. Lists of books, timetables, that sort of jazz. Her French, she believes, is coming back. Could we speak to someone so she can skip the English classes? The school lunch had been great. 'First course, a small piece of fish, like salmon, or a sardine, though it wasn't either. Second course, this big, spicy sausage, barely warm, but all right. We sit eight to a table and these women serve us from trolleys. Third course, lentils in a thick brown sauce. Great flavour and warmer than the sausage. Fourth course, grapes. There's a big basket of bread. The drink was apple juice. Everyone said it was cider but it wasn't alcoholic and it wasn't fizzy. I say it was apple juice.'

Kate and Polly describe their lunch in a rush, both speaking at once, but the consensus is as follows. 'Sort of vegetable soup with strands, weeds – they looked like grass but you could eat them – and little cubes of sort of like semolina. Nice apart from the semolina, having those soggy white chunks in your mouth. Then a chunk of meat, it might have been pork. Mine had too much fat but *brilliant*, in a sauce, only there weren't any seconds. Next lovely curly noodles in a cheese sauce. Then a petit suisse. They'd been on the table all the time and after everyone'd had one there were two left so we had them. No one else wanted them. The bread was stale. We had water but the teachers had wine. They had cheese too, real cheese, not just petit suisse. They all got their courses before we did. They're at a big table in the middle of the room and anyone naughty has to get up and stand on this chair. There wasn't any time the chair wasn't empty. We didn't have to stand on it ever.'

An improvement, the consensus agrees, on the tinned spaghetti and jam roll and custard at school in London, though to be fair to London, lunches there were half the price of Cahors lunches.

We should have guessed. The simple signature-signing that registered the girls into school is not all that is required. Evening after evening they return to the flat with forms to fill out and requests for money due. Insurance forms, health forms, sports activity forms, lunch forms, unintelligible teachers' or possibly parents' trade union forms. The French public schools system is free but the incidentals add up.

The weeks slide by. Lucy returns from school muttering about her quantities of devoir, homework. 'The maths is vectors. They're little arrows which are supposed to be a way of getting from one point to another, and I don't understand them.' 'To the vector belongs the spoils,' I say. The young need to be encouraged.

'History is the sans culottes and I don't know who they are. They're people without knickers in the French Revolution. History's so boring, the teacher just writes all this stuff on the blackboard and we copy it down. Geography, we have to trace maps of the USA and the USSR and colour in the cities and rivers and oil refineries and nuclear power stations. For Latin I've got to translate Caesar from French into Latin. All Caesar's battle plans and for ever moving into winter quarters.' She shuts herself in her room with her devoir and Led Zeppelin.

Kate and Polly come home with vocabulary lists to be learned by heart. They listen to Joan Baez songs and Simon and Garfunkel. They saunter round Cahors, looking in shop windows, and feeding bread to the swans in the park. They believe they may be in love with one of their classmates, a sloe-eyed lad named Taufik, or Staufik, they're not sure which.

3 Armistice Day

T HE DAYS shorten, the weather grows cool and rainy, and for weeks on end a fair of dreadful gaudiness and din rocks the Allées Fénelon, where in more tranquil times men play boules under the chestnut trees. The fair attracts evening gangs of the unseemliest elements of Cahors, Kate and Polly prominent among them. Seldom having money to spend, these two are present mainly as observers, as on a fact-finding mission for the United Nations. The fact they hope to find is the presence in the sweaty crush of their damson-eyed classmate, Taufik.

Lucy is too advanced for such vulgarity. Anyway she has loads and loads of simply impossible homework. When she does attend the fair with her pals she drives her bumper car as if she were at war.

The price of tomatoes climbs. Melons have vanished until next melon season. The melons were splendid but enough is enough. I'm content to say goodbye to them not least because I still haven't learned how to choose one. Everybody else in Cahors knows how, though they all disagree. Watch the French at melon time. Some scrutinize the melon for discoloured, squishy patches. Others weigh it in one hand, rap it with a knuckle, rattle it against an ear, press it with a thumb, or perform combinations of these. The food correspondent for *Le Monde*, France's best and often dullest newspaper (no photos, for one thing, just like the *Wall Street Journal*), writes, 'A good sign of ripeness is the appearance, at the opposite end from the stem, of a large pigmented ring reminiscent of the areola of a woman's breast.'

Too bad that this advice appeared in Le Monde in 1991. Had I known in the seventies that what I should have been looking for was a large pigmented ring reminiscent of the areola of a woman's breast, I might have become an accomplished melon-selector.

Before the local plums vanish too, I make twelve kilos of plum jam, in batches, each batch burning anew the bottom of the pan. Polly has such a passion for plum jam that our lives will be made wretched if she doesn't have a steady supply. I'm also six chapters into the fiction-in-progress, which isn't bad considering the distractions.

Catherine is holding English conversation classes twice a week at the cultural centre. Lucy has taken up yoga and drama. Kate and Polly, filled with plum jam, have joined both the swimming club and the gymnastics club. These occupy them every weekday evening, while on Sunday a bus sweeps them off to compete against far-flung Montauban, Toulouse, and Figeac. (Figeac: birthplace of (a) Champollion, the Egyptologist who deciphered the Rosetta Stone, and (b) Charles Boyer, smouldering lover of the silver screen who looked not unlike Napoleon, played him opposite Garbo in Marie Walewska, but was usually saying 'Darlink' to Dietrich – The Garden of Allah – or to Hedy Lamarr – Algiers – to name but two darlinks.) Kate and Polly do not win their swimming and gymnastics competitions but neither do they come last. With the smugness of Olympic athletes they have brought home runner-up medals.

Hallowe'en passes without our noticing. No one here notices Hallowe'en and they have naturally never heard of Guy Fawkes Night. Instead we notice Toussaint, November 1, a national holiday honouring all the saints, when families visit the cemeteries with flowers. The market area at the foot of the rue Joffre is filled with flower sellers. Hothouse flowers, plastic flowers. We bump into sceptical Monsieur Foissac, the schoolmaster from Catus.

'C'est le commerce,' he growls. As often as not the flowers brought to the cemeteries are chrysanthemums, being in season. In London we were as likely to present a hostess with chrysanthemums as with any other flower, and now, invited to supper at the home of new French acquaintances, we bring chrysanthemums. The flowers are received graciously but not swooned over. Afterwards, when we think about it, our host and hostess seemed nonplussed. Many months and gifts of chrysanthemums later we learn that chrysanthemums are not given as a gift in France. Chrysanthemums signify death and are for graves.

Talking of graves, we also notice November 11, Armistice Day. My father survived four years in France with the Royal Artillery, in the Great War, as he called it, and lived another fifty-five years as a civil engineer building roads, bridges, and a fine sewage plant at Windsor. He was so proud of the sewage plant that he came close to insisting I go with him to see it, he who seldom insisted on anything. To please him I went anyway. I was less thrilled with the sewage plant than he was but as such constructions go it may well have been first rate. He led me along walkways through flat acres of grass, channels of water, and immense concrete discs, some of them possibly rotating, though memory is fuzzy. The air was fresh, seagulls mewled overhead, and that was about it. (You don't often see seagulls in Windsor. They must have arrived for a tour, like myself.)

Anyway, every July 1 at breakfast, before whipping off the top of the first of his two soft-boiled eggs, my father would matter-of-factly remark, 'Today, 1916 – seven in the morning, breakfast time – the British and French attacked on the Somme. By evening, nineteen thousand British dead. Another forty thousand wounded or prisoners.' I believe he would have announced this had my mother, brother, me, or anyone at all, not been present.

He could quote, though he didn't, the number of French and German dead, and the casualties of all nationalities. He knew who and how many died at, say, Ypres – Wipers, he pronounced it – the length of the British line from Arras

32

to the Oise (68 miles) which 62 German divisions assaulted on March 21, 1918, and a welter of military minutiae from August 4, 1914, his birthday, and the day Britain went to war with Germany, to Armistice Day. His favourite reading was regimental histories of World War One, the more detailed and drier the better. 'I like them dry,' he would say. He did not want deathless prose, or poetry, though he would occasionally recite Siegfried Sassoon's poem about the general – the 'cheery old card' – whose plan of attack did for Harry and Jack as they slogged up from Arras with rifle and pack. He liked figures, comparative tables of armaments, and fold-out maps. Naval histories too he enjoyed. He knew the precise deployment of the high-seas fleets at Jutland. He would sometimes say a little wistfully, amused at himself, that he would have liked to have 'gone to sea'. He owned an impressive, complete Conrad, bound in blue leather, which he recommended me to read, especially the sea stories. I was fifty before I read Conrad. If my Dad hadn't recommended him I would have got to him much sooner. Too bad, the rebelliousness of youth, but if an engineer liked Conrad, how could I?

My father did not own many books, he borrowed from the library, but one he possessed and returned to for entire evenings was on Scottish tartans. Open the book anywhere, on the glossy left-hand page a colour plate of a tartan, and on the right a text giving the history of the clan. Why tartans enchanted him was a mystery to me. He was from Lancashire, he didn't have a drop of Scottish blood. His only connection with Scotland was a brother who happened to live there. I now wonder if his interest might not be traced back to World War One. When he received the king's shilling he was ordered to the Royal Scots Greys, or the Black Watch – I forget what regiment but it was Scottish – and for some months he was knocked into shape by Scotsmen before being shunted off to the Royal Artillery. In the Scots Guards, or similar, he was mounted, which is to say, put on a horse. After being transferred out of the Scottish regiment, never again did he sit on a horse. But if horses failed to win his

33

affection, he may have kept a soft spot for the regiment and matters Scottish.

He certainly retained the army's obsession with having your shoes mirror-bright. Shoe cleaning on the kitchen table was a ceremony. Sheets of newspaper spread out, Cherry Blossom polish to the right, brushes just so. I once asked him why he always cleaned the bottom of his shoes, the arched area between the sole and heel which no one would see except the worms in the grass he walked on at the sewage plant. Habit, he said. At inspection in the Gordon Highlanders, as it may have been, on horseback, you had to lift your feet to the inspecting officer's gaze. Not only did the whole stirrup have to dazzle, including the bit you had your foot on, but the bottom of the boot itself.

He was never gripped by World War Two as he was by the Great War. I suspect he would have liked to return to uniform but the Ministry Of Aircraft Production summoned him to build runways.

He was a fan of France (he read every Simenon story he could lay his hands on) but not of French champagne. At weddings, the only occasion when champagne came his way – he much preferred beer – he would observe in his Lancashire accent, 'One thing about champagne, you can't shave with it. It won't lather.' Once in his Great War he had been trapped for three days with some mates in the cellar of a destroyed restaurant, shells bursting overhead, and no liquid to shave with except hundreds of bottles of champagne – Veuve Cliquot, Taitinger, that brand of stuff. None of the champagnes would produce a lather.

After that war he took a degree in physics at Manchester University. The big event one term was to be a lecture by Einstein, admission by ticket only. My Dad and his pals, physics students, automatically received tickets. They arrived in good time at the lecture hall but already it was packed. They had to stand at the back, fortunately as it turned out. Onto the platform walked the head of the physics department, with perhaps the Lord Mayor of Manchester, and himself, Albert Einstein, wild, wiry hair pointing every which way. He would have been fortyish and either had just won the Nobel prize or was about to win it. The head of the department introduced him. Einstein stood and began his address. He spoke entirely in German. My Dad and his chums sidled out of the lecture hall and round the corner to the pub.

A widower for his last five years, he died a year before his younger son and the family caravan trundled into Cahors. Had he lived he would surely have visited us there, walked and talked a great deal, enjoyed the bread and cheese, and mildly grumbled at the absence of flat, warm, tasty, pub beer. Had he visited in November he would have walked to the Armistice Day service.

So, sixty years on from his war, November 11 draws some sixty or so people to the war memorial in Cahors: the last veterans of 1914–1918, widows and children of those who died, compulsory local politicians, a newspaper reporter, a camera, and passers-by. We hear speeches from our elected representatives, from the mayor, and from a priest a prayer. A wreath is laid, a squad of soldiers fire their rifles at the sky. The brief proceedings are as simple and moving as in Britain. How could they not be? *Sunt lacrimae rerum*. Britain lost three-quarters of a million men in World War One, France almost double that, and Germany suffered worst of all. According to my Dad that war was 'a good war' – no Nazis I think he meant – and he never bore Germany any grudge. A tiny band plays the *Marseillaise*, closing the ceremony.

I almost typed 'tinny'. In fact the band plays not badly. The *Marseillaise* is recognizable. This is unusual and meritorious. Part of the French cultural tradition is that a town band should perform as if none of its members had ever before held a musical instrument. They are expected to play execrably and usually succeed. Nothing chauvinistic intended. Amateur bands of other nations sound perhaps equally wretched, always excepting Yorkshire and Lancashire's ruthlessly competitive brass bands – Brighouse and Rastrick, Black Dyke, Heckmondwyke Colliery – which sound like the Royal Philharmonic without the strings. From the discordant bleating of French town bands one would imagine the bandmaster responsible for leading the parade had handed out instruments to the first people he met on the street, children included.

Accompanied by small boys, girls, and dogs, the band marches down the Boulevard Gambetta playing what sounds as if it might be *My Old Kentucky Home*, though it's hard to be sure. They come to a ragged halt outside a café, break ranks, shake spittle from their bugles and tubas, and file into the café for refreshment.

Catherine has driven to Catus to order from Madame Becquet two ducks for confit de canard. The preserved duck in sealed jars will be ready for us next February or March, Madame says. We have watched her force-feed her ducks and geese to produce foie gras, the bird's neck between her knees, a funnel down its throat, the grain tipped in, so we don't need to see that again. She says the birds like it, they are being fed. Those that have been fed lie immobile, or if they do try to walk, waddle a couple of steps then flop down. I am reminded of a fox-hunting woman in County Cork who really did insist that the fox adores the thrill of the chase. The tricky part is that foie gras is one of the gustatory triumphs of western civilization. Best not talk about it.

The weather grows ever wetter and windier. We hear reports of the Lot flooding. Let it flood (not too much), we are settling in most cozily. What wastes time is having to pause at each pâtisserie window to goggle at the pastries and tarts in their subdued colours, or at each butcher's window, where the trimmed, cylindrical loin of beef is tied with circles of string, each string a meticulous four centimetres from the next. Every *alimentation* window brings on frothy salivation, reminiscent of Harrods' food department. Too bad there are no crusty, gelatinous pork pies here.

No pork pies and no public library. London has magnificent public libraries, as do the provinces. Here, nothing. It isn't as if the French don't read. They do. I can't imagine what I had hoped for because if Cahors did have a public library the books would be in French. All the same, a blow. Friends from across the Channel will visit. They will bring books and pork pies.

Here is the good news. Did we or did we not, the other day, hear Kate and Polly being cross with each other in an approximation of French?

In the flat we turn on the central heating.

4 Meeting the Locals

T WO INDIVIDUALS in particular ease the settling-in process during these first months in Cahors. They are Taufik, the small, tough, beautiful Tunisian boy beloved by Kate and Polly – that is about all I ever learn of Taufik – and Gustave (let us call him), an energetic history teacher and left-wing politician.

Gustave Gaillac has an office in the Mairie, the Town Hall, a wife who knows and sings all the yearning, dated French songs that I know, plus many more, and five children. The younger children are Lucy's age, two being twins and a tad wild. One Saturday, Cahors crammed with market stalls – not just food but clothing, china, trinket jewellery, gramophone records, and a man on a box barking out the virtues of his herbal remedies, most of them for digestive ailments – one of the twins dresses as a priest and stalks the Boulevard Gambetta making the sign of the cross and telling people, 'Bless you, my child'.

Gustave is lean and fit, apart from a bad back. He is a jogger, of whom France has not a lot (France has bicyclists), and a member of the town's new Association France-Grande Bretagne. Until recently Cahors and environs did not have enough Brits to warrant an Association France-Grande Bretagne. Now it seems we are sufficient and suddenly the Association exists, not that Catherine and I have come to the Lot to meet Brits. Gustave says he would like to learn English but I don't believe him. That's to say, I believe he would like to know English, but he'll never learn it, not from us anyway. He is too busy guiding us in clear French through France's bureaucratic swamp and showing us how we fill in social security forms, child allowance forms, tax forms, and writers' and teachers' union forms, none of which we would have a clue about but for Gustave. He knows the short-cuts through officialdom and is a personal friend of the officials. On our behalf he makes telephone calls and stands in line at the tax office and the prefecture.

French bureaucracy, in spite of a reputation for rigidity, obstructionism, indifference, and joy in rendering complex what ought to be simple, is no worse than other bureaucracies I have come up against. Unless I'm naive, it is not corrupt. Money doesn't change hands before you have your resident's permit stamped or buy a train ticket. But knowing the right people does no harm, and when you know everybody, as Gustave does, you pick up the phone, speak passingly of the grape harvest, drop a couple of names, and your documents are as good as stamped. Nothing unlawful. Favours are granted, favours are received. How else could life go on?

'It's not knowing what, it's knowing who,' my Dad would say. Goodness, enough. He'd have been so embarrassed to see himself quoted.

Perhaps a bottle of Cahors wine changes hands. A tin of foie grass. We don't inquire.

Gustave also takes under his wing, unless they very sensibly put themselves there, a family in direr straits than ours. Jeffrey and Sally Stride have brisk French but no money. They are artists so committed to painting that they won't do anything else, such as teach painting, and therefore cannot reasonably expect to have any money until after they are dead. He is English, she Welsh, both are musical, both skinny, except Sally when she's pregnant, and though poor as church mice they are buoyant. We sense tension only over whose turn it is to paint, whose to entertain the children. They need every crumb that France's generous welfare state has to offer and will find the crumbs more readily with Gustave showing them how to go about it.

They are here because they were driving round France, painting, and here is where their car expired, they say. They live outside Cahors in whatever farmhouse or abandoned schoolhouse happens to be available at a peppercorn rent. When we first meet they are growing their own vegetables at a house with an outside toilet and so far off any known road that it can't be found, you have to be led there. Idyllic in summer, rough in winter. They paint the landscape. When they sell a painting they repay a chunk to the bank and withhold what remains for a celebratory visit to Cahors, the market, friends, us (depositing the children while they jaunt off to the shops), perhaps even a restaurant.

The children so far are – One: Sebastian, aged four or five, insufferably talkative but distractable by any intelligent game. (He will become a chess champion, shuttling off to junior chess tournaments all over France.) Two: his very small sister, Rosa, calm with a runny nose. One day the Catus schoolteacher couple are lunching with us in the rue Joffre when the Strides pop in. Under the table Sebastian bites the schoolmaster's leg. 'Aaaagh!' cries the schoolmaster. 'Sebastian, don't do that,' says Jeff, and carries on talking about a group exhibition in Paris where he will be showing his paintings.

Jeff plays the violin and anything that comes to hand. Catherine has acquired a battered, unplayable tuba of a bygone era, an objet trouvé for decoration, though it will need strenuous polishing. Jeff puts it to his lips and pumps out *Happy Birthday to You*, a solo far too accurate to qualify him for the town band. At his first encounter with a touch-tone telephone he plays *God Save the Queen*. We wonder if this sets the telephones ringing in Buckingham Palace. He has an infuriating habit of tunelessly humming, on and on. When I tackle him about this, asking if he might not secretly be tone deaf, he says he's humming the tenor part of the Brahms *Requiem*. Sally, pianist, paints landscapes which vibrate with colour. Customers discuss whether they prefer a Sally to a Jeff. In winter when the snow piles up they paint interiors and portraits. One sunny lunchtime on their terrace I am climbing over debris to reach the table when Jeff shouts, 'Don't touch the deckchair!' He is painting the deckchair. 'Have you ever looked at a deckchair, really looked?' he wants to know.

Since he asks, no, I can't say I have. But I know the French for a deckchair. I've known it since school. *Une transatlantique*. It's the unlikeliest words that stick.

Jim and Peggy Wolfe are a retired English couple who live a civilized life in a restored farmhouse with a swimming pool and two outsize, untrainable, thoroughbred dogs. Their bedside books are Pepys and Boswell. Both wear classic tweeds. Peggy puts on an excellent meal of steak and kidney pudding, jam roll, and red wine. Jim walks the dogs but never far enough. In the house the dogs are two whirlwinds, knocking over furniture, their master and mistress, and visitors. I don't recall the breed, something no one has heard of. Jim and Peggy say the dogs have so much energy because they are still puppies. Does this mean they are still growing? In the end the dogs have to be found homes on farms where the family is fond and resilient enough not to mind being knocked down. Visiting Jim and Peggy is a pleasure once the dogs have left. The road to their house is uphill and sinuous. Returning to Cahors requires especial care. You keep a foot on the brake or you could go off the road. When we next meet Jim and Peggy in these pages they will be in their car with house guests but off the road and upside down.

French being Taufik's first language we cannot understand why he is with Kate and Polly in Monsieur Spiaggi's integrating class. Perhaps the headmaster needed six in the class to justify its existence and picked Taufik's name from his hat. Kate and Polly have no complaint. If they pass Taufik on the street they make kissing noises at him. In the school yard a group some ten strong, Taufik, Kate and Polly among them,

41

play gendarmes et voleurs, the point being for one team to dash across the playground and touch the wall without being caught by the opposing team. On one dash Polly is caught and encircled by boys, including Taufik. She is so hot she peels off her pinafore, forgetting that underneath she wears only tights. She stands there, most wretched of females, then hauls the pinafore back on. Ah, the mortifications of childhood! The shame does nothing to quench Polly's ardour for Taufik.

Though the lad is pointed out to me often enough across a crowded boulevard, I meet him only once. I'm retrieving Kate and Polly from the swimming pool and find I have a flat tyre. *Un pneu crevé*. (*Pneu* is a fine word to say because you explode the p, or at any rate pronounce it, which we don't with our dismal pneumatic and pneumonia.) With nudgings and whisperings, Kate and Polly reveal that over there is Taufik, and why not ask him to help change the tyre, because he knows about that sort of thing.

Taufik is a mere eleven but I have no pride when it comes to tyre-changing. I'm not saying he changed the tyre entirely by himself, only that without him I might have been changing it well into the night. Equally praiseworthy, and unlike some yobs hereabouts, he refrains from sniggering at our English registration, HLM. An HLM, *habitation louée modérée*, is a cheap council house. All in all I am favourably impressed with Taufik. We shake begrimed hands and I drive off with the girls. As long as Taufik employs his hands for such purposes as changing tyres I shall continue to offer him every courtesy.

Who else?

I must invent a name for the blue-blood whose acquaintance we make if only because I never learn his full name, which will be equivalent to the strings of names for dukes and earls in *Burke's Peerage*. Hubert d'Argentat, let's say. He is an authentic French aristocrat, or would be but for 1789, offspring of, say, the eleventh marquis Gilles Florival Fleury Alembert Dagobert Guignol d'Argentat. Monsieur Argentat is a good-looking family man who, two and a half centuries ago, might have been found periwigged at the court of Versailles. In France's Fifth Republic he is a minor civil servant working in an office in Cahors. As he has never learned to drive he walks the two miles to his office each morning, walks home for lunch at noon, walks back to the office for the afternoon session, and walks home again in the evening. Monsieur Argentat is a fervent royalist, determined that the monarchy be restored as the one divinely-ordained government of France. On weekends, tieless and wearing a dishevelled raincoat, he boards local trains and patrols the corridors, entering each compartment to hand out royalist tracts. If a compartment is empty he leaves tracts on the seats.

We first meet him at a social gathering where he insists that everyone play bridge, though nobody wants to. He considers himself the bridge champion of south-west France. In fact he plays extremely poorly, at times making up his own rules. One afternoon he comes into our flat without knocking and bearing a thick manuscript which details the derivation and historical significance of every street name in Cahors, his own work of many years' labour, and quite possibly of value. He wants me to translate and edit it for the British market. Convincing Monsieur Argentat that this would involve months of work, even were my French up to it, takes one hour, after which he is unconvinced but departs anyway, leaving the door open. Should he return I shall be sorely tempted to puff pipe smoke in his face.

On an occasion at his home, Monsieur Argentat shows Catherine a number of avant-garde paintings that he has executed with paint, toothpaste, and shoe polish. Diplomatic to the last, Catherine evades giving an opinion by remarking, 'They must give you great pleasure to do.'

'On the contrary,' says Monsieur Argentat, 'I detest painting. I paint only to show my family that I have the talent.'

Ginette has no blue blood but she has grace and perfect manners. She is a cultured, devoted wife and mother of middle age, petite, attractive, law-abiding, home-loving, and utterly uneccentric, or so I'd have supposed, though given to moments of bizarre humour. Her husband, Raymond, a retired government scientist, is converting a wing of their château, ten miles from Cahors, into a self-contained flat where they will be able to escape the racket of grown children and grandchildren on holiday. 'Our mouroir', Ginette calls it. A mouroir is a place where people go to die.

Ginette has decided she will visit London where two of her daughters are working. She has never been to London and were it not for her daughters would never dream of going, but she misses them. She insists that she will survive the five days away from home and her husband's sawing and hammering in the mouroir. For economy she opts for the train and cross-Channel ferry. Such are her pre-travel organizings, telephonings, and anxieties, she might be setting off for the Solomon Islands. A major anxiety is her lack of English. She comes to the rue Joffre with an English-French phrase book published in 1906 for session number one of a crash course from Catherine. After the lesson she abandons the project with a sigh.

We arrive at Cahors railway station to wish Ginette bon voyage. She stands rigidly on the platform with her suitcases, comforted by Raymond. Raymond is looking forward to five days of bachelor freedom in which he will fortify his food with the abundance of garlic forbidden by Ginette. The train accelerates Ginette away into the unknown. The next afternoon she is back in Cahors.

That she progressed no further than Boulogne is due not to a failure of nerve but to a difficulty over her carte d'identité, the yellow identity card with photograph, personal details, signature, and official stamp, that is carried by all French adults. Ginette's identity card expired twenty-two years ago. Aware this might present a problem, two days before setting out she had attempted to sort the matter out with an inquiry at the préfecture, where she learned that renewal of an identity card takes at least a week. She pressed on anyway. At Boulogne, where police cast cursory glances at identity cards, Ginette's stood out by being not yellow but faded blue, a museum piece. All that was correct about Ginette's identity card was her name. The edges had been trimmed to conform to current dimensions, the photograph had been doctored with pencil, and the original dates had been scratched out and new dates inserted.

All might still have been well had her policeman been the sort who hands back the identity card saying, 'Carry on this time, Madame, but be sure to renew it first thing when you return home.' Her misfortune was to be confronted by the other sort of policeman. Before putting her on the train back to Paris, thence Cahors, he lectured her and impugned her morals. Loyal to the last, Ginette forbore to reveal that the tampering and forging had been the work of her husband. Not that that would have cut any ice with this policeman. One started out with crimes one might consider minor, such as falsifying legal documents, he informed Ginette. The next step was drugs. After drugs, the streets. A life of vice, Madame. She had taken the first step. Ahead lay unimaginable sordidness. Prison, the loss of dignity, friends, family, and an early death.

Ten days later, armed with a shiny yellow identity card with no scratchings-out and pencillings-in, Ginette visits London. She returns heady with excitement, with news of her daughters and of a world beyond her beloved Lot. She is not saying she must return to London next week or ever. There were cultural differences, bewilderments, she tells us. Englishmen particularly. Why did they not notice her?

Not long ago, in the early nineties, France's then prime minister, Edith Cresson, made the front page of Britain's newspapers with an observation that Anglo-Saxon men are not interested in women. She remembered from strolling in the streets of London that men did not look at her, whereas in Paris they do. A woman columnist for the Daily Telegraph agreed that in an English street a woman might as well have a paper bag over her head for all the notice any man will take. This is what Ginette was saying when she returned from London fifteen years ago.

45

'The Englishmen, you Britishers, why do they not look at me?' she wants to know. 'Here in France the men look at me. Why not in London? Am I so ugly?' She is casting bait, hoping to catch a compliment. I assure her that the English males did look at her, but discreetly. Perhaps we are shy, possibly more subtle than the French. Incontestably she was looked at, with delight, everywhere, but with respect for her privacy, not blatantly.

'Bon, I thought that was it,' Ginette says, smiling, head high, as she walks to the kitchen to prepare a pot of camomile tea.

The glowingest gem in the crown of Cahors, French or English, is Elizabeth Espitalié. She happens to be English, from the Home Counties – Ashford, Kent, I believe – Betjeman-land, where lupins bloom kemptly in gardens, laburnum flanks gravelled driveways, and Miss Joan Hunter Dunn and her subaltern, after the golf club dance, sit in the car-park till twenty-to-one. Elizabeth is a rosy-cheeked enthusiast with a spirited laugh and generous heart. Her severest criticism of anyone is 'Silly old badger'. As often as not she is putting up visitors at her home on the Avenue de Toulouse, a mile from the centre of Cahors, hostess to Brits who are friends of friends, young people who may have met one of her children (two boys, two girls) and haven't the money for a hotel, and many a Scot. Elizabeth is the elected president of the Association France-Grande Bretagne. The association holds an occasional Sunday lunch for its members at a country restaurant, followed by a hike across the *causses*, the chalky hills of the Lot. It puts on book sales and jumble sales – All Contributions Welcome – in the plate-glass gallery by the town tourist bureau, and organizes exchanges with Dumfries, Scotland, twin town of Cahors. Catherine will find herself boarding the chartered coach for Dumfries, and in Cahors we shall be host to Scottish lads and lassies who arrive paper-white and shy and depart two weeks later fire-engine red and shy.

Elizabeth's French is rapid, accurate – she tosses her head, laughs, and denies the accuracy – and delivered with a fine Oxford accent. Her Home Counties French is the only swift French I have ever understood. I understood De Gaulle but he spoke paralysingly slowly and simply. ('Français, Françaises, aidez-moi!') She is married to a Frenchman, Jean, no less precious a jewel, who speaks English but prefers French. Jean is French down to his beret, shrugs, scepticism, wry humour, and taking for granted that whatever else mealtime might offer there will be bread and red wine, bread especially. Breadcrumbs bestrew the carpet at Jean's feet at lunch and supper. He is a whiz car mechanic with his own business. He services our Renault, though he'd be happier servicing something challenging, a veteran Sunbeam or Bentley. But he is selling his garage to Opel because they want to buy it and he is ready for a change. He switches from employer to employee, driving rental cars back to base from wherever they have been deposited. Cahors to Lyons. Marseilles to Cahors. Bordeaux to Limoges.

Too bad but we don't meet Jean and Elizabeth until we are deep into November, and when we do we don't immediately follow up. As I say, we are not in Cahors to meet Brits. Anyway, too late to invite them to our American Thanksgiving dinner.

Our what? Read on.

5 An American Thanksgiving

H OW CAN we think about celebrating Thanksgiving in the Lot with not an American in sight, no American flag, no pecans for decorating the pumpkin pie, not even a piano for picking out the song about spacious skies and purple mountains' majesty above the fruited plain? Catherine and I are not American. We haven't even seen America for a dozen years. But we enjoy Thanksgiving. The fourth Thursday of November seldom passes without our celebrating this friendliest of festivals (never are there tantrums at Thanksgiving, unlike Christmas) with American friends, or American friends of friends, in London, Ireland, Jersey, or wherever we happen to find ourselves.

We wonder if it makes sense, may not indeed be presumptuous, for non-Americans to celebrate Thanksgiving in the Lot without the presence of a single American. We have heard of an American couple who own a house in the hills not far away, but they spend most of the year touring places like Ecuador and Sumatra, and anyway we have not been introduced. We should surely elbow Thanksgiving this time round, or at most settle for a quiet turkey and pumpkin pie for the five of us.

We remember that Kate is American. This always comes as a surprise. She has lived only briefly in America, aged zero to six months, but she was born in Illinois while I was teaching there so she's American. Kate the Yank. She has somewhere not only a birth certificate as evidence but a flamboyant scroll from the hospital bearing her hours-old footprints. We will go ahead with Thanksgiving, no question. We will have Hamlet without the prince but with French princelings in lieu, though probably not Monsieur Argentat, the royalist. We will invite French friends and educate them in this peculiarly American feast. We will bring the conversation round to Lafayette and Jean Lafite and raise our glasses to them – I personally shall not toast those enemies of the British crown, but I will make no issue of our French guests doing so.

We break the news to the children. 'I shall be out,' says Lucy. Lucy is at a stage where her parents can do little right. The only adults more embarrassing than her parents are her parents' friends. As determined party buffs Kate and Polly show more enthusiasm, but less than might have been hoped, distracted as they are by Taufik. The heck with them. Catherine and I are in the grip of pre-Thanksgiving euphoria.

We will invite our new friends the Radiguets. They are an aristocratic, birdlike widow and her marriageable daughter, Marie-Claude, not that we have anyone to marry her to. We shall ask the Foissacs, Catus schoolteachers, and their small son, who attends judo classes three evenings a week. Also Gustave Gaillac, who as a history teacher will be excited by an occasion marking an historic event, the first harvest brought in by the *Mayflower* pilgrims, in Plymouth, Massachusetts, in 1621. Gustave, his wife and five teenage children, and ourselves, brings the total to seventeen, which is enough. We have barely sufficient crockery and cutlery for ourselves, let alone a dozen guests, but we will manage. Had not those first American colonists managed?

We put Kate and Polly to work designing invitations. (Lucy has made a strategic disappearance.) Polly draws and colours a horse for one invitation and a Christmas tree for another. Kate assaults magazines with scissors. Failing to find pilgrims and sheaves of wheat she produces a collage of a pair of lips, a woman standing with one hand on a washing machine, and a Camembert. From *Larousse* we learn that the

French for Thanksgiving is Action de Grâces d'États-Unis, so we print that in the invitations so our guests will be aware this is no run-of-the-mill dinner party. We send off the invitations, including a request for the Gaillacs to bring a dozen knives, forks and spoons. Our bridges burned, we draw up a list of pluses and minuses.

The big plus is one untapped jar of cranberry sauce brought from London, which should be sufficient if the girls exercise a little FHB (Family Hold Back). Without it there would be head-scratching, *les airelles* – cranberries – being unknown in Cahors, fresh or tinned. All other ingredients for the dinner we believe to be available. Pumpkins are everywhere as are sweet potatoes. Though we can't recall seeing turkeys in the market, we have noticed chickens, ducks, geese, and guinea hens, so presumably there will be turkeys.

No minuses that seem insuperable. Besides assorted gas rings our kitchen has an Aga-like coal-burning stove and oven which are unusable because the chimney is blocked, but we have been intending to have it unblocked. If the chimney sweep fails us we can borrow Madame Radiguet's oven and run through the streets with the turkey and pumpkin pie while our assembled guests discuss Lafayette and Lafite. Thanksgiving mood music for the apéritif hour? All we have are the Brandenburg concertos two, four, and five, Kate's long-playing records of the Beatles and their ilk, Lucy's rock cacophanies, and a few inappropriate strays, sifting through which we come upon Polly's Burl Ives with such songs as *Jim Johnson's Mule* (I hear myself instructing the Gaillacs, 'Icons of early American history such as Cotton Mather and Jim Johnson . . .') and one about a whale: 'In San Francisco there lived a whale. She ate pork chops by the pail.'

The apéritif? Here's a challenge. What's the traditional drink to precede Thanksgiving dinner? We can't remember. Perhaps there is no traditional apéritif. But our guests will expect one. What would Cotton Mather and his black-suited elders have drunk? Water probably. Jim Johnson sounds like a moonshine man, which is no help. The French take a Pernod or Scotch or one of their fortified wines. We have been offered kir, and on classy evenings, champagne. In the most sophisticated circles, so we've been told, a straightforward glass of wine is très snob. But this is an occasion calling for something unequivocally American. I have a feeling eggnog might be American but Catherine believes eggnog is more for Christmas. Mint julep is American but we have no recipe. We have no recipe for anything American. Our few American recipe books are in London.

'Whiskey sours,' Catherine says.

Whiskey sours, of course! We have in the past scored a knockout success with whiskey sours, and the recipe we think we remember, near enough. Isn't it simply Bourbon whiskey, lemon juice, sugar, and ice? Without wishing to patronize our French guests, none of them is going to know. For the children a foolproof family lemonade: lemons, citric acid from the pharmacy, sugar, and plentiful water to dilute. Undiluted it is poisonous.

Apart from the shopping only two main matters remain outstanding. First, the carving knife must be professionally sharpened. How often have we been caught out by the carving knife! Brilliant company, imperishable wit, matchless table setting, cooking of a quality to bring down a benison from the ghost of Carême himself – and a carving knife as blunt as a stick, having served for sawing string and paper, mending electric plugs, and scraping fossilized toffee and gum from surfaces.

Second, the Stars and Stripes. We have to have flags. We tour the bookshops and toy shops with no success. We promise Kate and Polly money if they will scour the unvisited shops in the alleys leading to the river. They return hot and thrilled, demanding their money, having spotted the American flag across the back pocket of a pair of jeans in the Pantashop. So we do what we should have done in the first place, putting them to work at the kitchen table with their paints, the blank reverse side of unwanted posters, and the Stars and Stripes from which to copy. (Lucy has remembered a pressing engagement at a friend's house.)

51

The only illustration of the flag we can put our hands on is in the inside cover of *Larousse* wedged between Espagne and Ethiopie in a spread of 132 flags of the world. If you've tried making your own Stars and Stripes you will know that the flag is not complicated in a design sense, though there is no denying it lacks the simplicity of the Japanese flag or the Red Cross. But the Stars and Stripes is fiddling. All those stars. We count fifty – is that correct, fifty? Our *Larousse* is years out of date. Forty-eight is the number lodged in my mind since school days but I've a feeling Hawaii and Alaska have been added. Only Hawaii and Alaska? What about Puerto Rico?

'The French aren't going to know,' Catherine says, and we find ourselves eyeing each other, increasingly aware that we are banking on our French guests knowing very little. 'They may know,' she amends, 'but they're not going to count.'

We lend a hand with the red and white stripes. We make a smaller flag from a rectangle of old bedsheet and attach it to a knitting needle for planting in the turkey. Though I say it myself, the flags are a triumph: red, white, and blue and incontestably American. The colours have run on the bedsheet flag, giving a misty, Monet-esque effect. Of the two larger flags for the dining room wall one has thirty-four stars, the other close to sixty, but we agree that in the event that a guest is caught counting them we will distract him with a discussion of Lafayette and another whiskey sour.

We should have guessed that the requisite whiskey would be unobtainable. Cahors is not Paris. Scotch stands lined up on parade on the grocery shelves. No Bourbon though, or for that matter rye or Irish. Scotch sours? No, no. Why ruin a perfectly decent Scotch? We accept that the apéritif will have to be unimaginative Pernod and Dubonnet. Then, the day before Thanksgiving, in quest of shelled walnuts as a substitute for pecans, we venture into the exotic grocery in the rue Foch, an emporium we normally avoid because of its equally exotic prices. Skulking at the back of the topmost liquor shelf, dust-laden and unobserved since the GIs departed from France in 1945, are a bottle of Four Roses and a bottle of Kentucky Tavern. We buy the less pricey (whatever difference in quality there might be, our French guests aren't going to . . . et cetera) and jig back to the flat.

Fresh turkeys are not to be had and that's that. A week in advance we begin inquiries. The chain of inexpensive, reliable grocery stores is able to produce every kind of poultry except turkey. 'Too early, come back nearer Christmas,' the managers say. The covered market is equally blank: ducks, geese, chickens, guinea hens, quail, woodcock, dead, pathetic thrushes with their feathers on shot by local sportsmen, but no turkeys. We are met with amazement that anyone would want a turkey at this time of year, Christmas being only weeks away. In the Saturday market a vendor assures us, 'Turkeys will be starting soon. Possibly even next Saturday I might bring you a turkey.' Two days too late.

There is nothing for it but the cylindrical, oven-ready turkeys at the supermarket. They are not going to look the same when brought to the table, speared with the flag, but they are all meat, and after the whiskey sours no one will notice anyway. In Prisunic's food department we collect four two-pound *rôtis de dindonneau frais*, boned, rolled, encased in a trim layer of fat, and netted in mesh. Into the cart with the turkey we toss a pound of turkey sausages because they look good and we have never tried them. Also one large poule for the soup. *Poule effilée*, the label says. For simplicity's sake we want a gutted hen and hope *effilée* might mean that. *Effilé* normally means slender, tapered, sharp, thinned-out, which doesn't describe our hen at all, but with luck the word might be local usage for gutted and cleaned. Gutted is usually *vidé* for a fish and *étripé* for an animal, but none of the assorted fowl in front of us bears either term. Plucked would have been *plumé*, and all are that right enough, and tidily sealed in transparent paper. But which, if any, are cleaned? The frustration is trivial enough (Catherine once spent three months cleaning chickens on a farm in Denmark), but never once in France, here in the Lot or anywhere, have we lighted on a cleaned chicken, though we are assured they are available everywhere. We take the precaution of asking the woman in white overalls with the badge, though with no great confidence. Already we have asked for *gibiers* – giblets for the soup – whereupon she presented us with quail. (*Gibier* also means game so she wasn't altogether to be blamed.) Now she prods and shakes our *poule effilée* and assures us, yes, this hen is gutted. Back in the flat we find that it is nothing of the sort. They never are in France. I still don't know what *poule effilée* means and I no longer care.

This is the Tuesday before Thanksgiving. Every Thursday afternoon the chef, Catherine, walks ten miles o'er hill and dale with Ginette and Raymond, or Gustave, a habit she prefers not to break even for Thanksgiving. We polish off the bulk of the shopping: potatoes, flour, sugar, butter, lard, cornmeal for the spoon bread soufflé, celery and tomatoes for the soup, dried prunes, apricots and apples for the dried fruit pie, and lemons for the you-know-what. 'Don't worry, I'll have everything ready, you'll have very little to do,' the chef says.

We add paper plates, cups, napkins, and tablecloths. The table settings won't be exactly Georgian silver and damask but what counts, we agree, reflecting on the whiskey sours, is the spirit. We hesitate in front of the cheese counter.

'No,' say I. 'Do Americans eat cheese at Thanksgiving? They do not. This will be a dinner for the French to remember if only for the absence of cheese.'

Same with salad. We postpone the Brussels sprouts until the following day when they will be fresher in the midweek market. Pumpkin we have, a gross yellow wedge pressed on us by an acquaintance who grows them and is suffering from a private pumpkin mountain. As far as we can see from the checks on the shopping list we are all set.

The chimney sweep comes and goes. He almost goes to that happier land beyond in an avalanche of rubble. The oven

54

chimney is blocked not with soot but with debris from some past age when builders built a new roof and stuffed the old roof down the chimney. The chimney also has two kinks that laugh at our sweep's advanced equipment. Without going into details, let it simply be said that the morning of the sweep is hair-raising. The kitchen becomes filled with bricks and plaster, the roof trembles. The more Catherine and I beg the sweep to forget it, the more fiercely he fights. The chimney becomes a personal matter, a foe against which he batters and thrusts. He attacks it from below and from the roof. He rushes away and returns with heavier, even more formidable equipment. He is a young man, very determined, making his way in his career. Noon and the two-hour lunchtime are approaching, at which point a siren will wail from the Mairie, summoning all citizens to their tables, when we hear muffled screams that bring us racing to the kitchen. We see only our sweep's shoes at eye level. The rest of him is up the chimney. His screaming persists, each scream punctuated by a descent of rocks and brick dust. Gradually we interpret the screams as news that he has won. 'J'ai gagné, j'ai gagné!' he screams. What he can see is the sky. Raw-knuckled, disguised in plaster and cement, he descends. He sweeps up and departs with his terrifying equipment, delighted with his victory and leaving a paltry bill.

We set and light the stove oven. It works. We test it with baked potatoes and an apple pie. They work too. Nothing can stop us now.

On the eve of Thanksgiving Catherine cooks and prepares. She chops and dices with the professionally sharpened carving knife, and with a wine bottle in lieu of a rolling pin, one of various items of kitchen equipment we don't have, readies dough for the pies and for Irish soda bread (eaten at Thanksgiving by Irish-Americans if anyone asks). In the market the commis chef buys sprouts, sweet potatoes, and more pumpkin. By midmorning on Thanksgiving Day we are ahead of the game. Then the oven dies.

Also we are an essential baking dish short, and a new shopping list – so much for the checks on that first shopping list – is extending minute by minute. Sugar for lemonade, Gruyère for Mornay sauce for the sprouts, French bread in case Irish soda bread comes as too much of a shock to the delicate sensibilities of the French, peppercorns, an additional paper tablecloth, walnuts because the earlier batch has been discovered and eaten by the girls, and potatoes because since the sweep's triumph we have been on a baked potato binge and supplies have run low. Candles too. These are not a refinement but a necessity. The only possible room for dinner for seventeen is Kate's gigantic bedroom where the sole illumination is a naked bedside light.

While Catherine rackets off in the car to borrow a baking dish, the commis clears, sets and lights the stove, then steps out once more, flagging somewhat, with shopping basket. In Prisunic the first Christmas activities are under way. On a liquor stand speckled with glitter is Bourbon whiskey, the same brands we found in the exotic grocery but cheaper.

The oven heats up. 'Surely we're all right,' the chef says doubtfully. She has the baking dish. 'If you could just dust around, do the tables, I'll be back by six, time to do the spoon bread soufflé.' The guests are invited for seven. She disappears for her rendezvous and hike, leaving the commis in command.

A law of party giving states that such chores as dusting around and doing the tables, not to mention numberless more vital preparations, expand to fill the time available. The whiskey sours and lemonade are still to be made, flags to be affixed to the dining-room wall, and record player to be set up in the apéritif room. Chairs must be brought from the Mairie (a borrowing arranged by Gustave) if a third of the guests are not to be seated back-to-back on Kate's bed. Sprouts are to be washed and notched, potatoes to be peeled, candles and condiments put out, and cranberry sauce transferred from its jar to cocotte dishes. The kitchen, where guests will arrive and again pass through from apéritifs to dinner, requires more than dusting. On my knees, scrubbing and swabbing, I recall that the French take cube sugar in coffee – I have yet to meet the French person who drinks unsweetened coffee – and we

56

have only granulated and confectioner's sugar. Well, tough on that French habit.

At six the chef races back into the flat. The commis is seated at the kitchen table testing the whiskey sours and correcting the souvenir menus, wondering which way the accent goes on céleri. Back from school, Kate and Polly are writing place cards for the two dinner tables and disputing who will be placed where. (Lucy, pleading homework, has retired to her room.)

'How is it?' cries the chef, pink-cheeked and lame from the march through the hills.

'Just a touch more, I would hazard, of the Old Snakebite,' says the commis, pouring and testing.

The chef throws off boots and coat and hurls into action. 'What time are they coming? They'll not be on time, will they? It's impolite to be on time.'

'With possibly the merest hint more lemon for zest,' opines the commis.

Thirty minutes to go, and the commis in the bath, a squeal sounds from the kitchen. The cornmeal for the spoon bread soufflé has been discovered to be not cornmeal (semoule de maïs) but corn flour (fleur de maïs). The commis hurtles from the bath and into party clothes, testing the whiskey sour for zest en route, then into the night on his knees for semoule de maïs.

The exotic grocery comes up with it. The chef flings together a new spoon bread soufflé then flees for her bath. Time remains for adjustments to the whiskey sour. Polly is playing *Greensleeves* on her recorder, Kate is playing *Sweet Betsy from Pike* on hers, and from Lucy's homework room, whither she has smuggled the record player, issue rock thumpings.

At four minutes past seven Madame Radiguet and Marie-Claude arrive bearing gifts.

Looking back we are fairly sure that our Anglo-Irish-English-Franco-American Thanksgiving was a success, even a succès fou. But an odd aspect of dinner parties is that although everything may be ready on time (just), Party A might have host and hostess toiling like scullions while Party B is a breeze, for reasons impossible to discover. For chef and commis at this Thanksgiving in Cahors the only relatively relaxed spell is during the apéritif hour, which stretches to two hours, then to two and a half. Hard on the heels of the Radiguets arrive the Gaillacs, seven of them, also bearing gifts.

The gifts are for Catherine and Kate: mimosa, several books, a cake, chocolates, and a five-hundred-piece jigsaw of the Pont Valentré. From out of the handshaking, embracing, and mysterious congratulations to Catherine and Kate we gather that this day is the feast of St Catherine, or Saint Katherine. We also gather that the Radiguets, if not the Gaillacs, believe the purpose of the dinner is to honour the feast day of Saint Catherine, about whom nothing certain is known. She may have lived in the fourth century, possibly was learned, was condemned to death on the wheel, saved by a miracle, but later beheaded. Her name was dropped from the liturgical calendar in 1969. Heaven knows how our guests had interpreted Action de Grâces d'États-Unis on the invitation, if they had read it.

Catherine explains Thanksgiving while I tour with the jug of whiskey sour. The apéritif arouses interest and is declined only by Marie-Claude, who has a cold. Madame Radiguet is deeply moved by Catherine's account of that first harvest in the New World, interrupting with questions, and when the lesson seems to be over, launching into a narrative of her own experience of the United States, a week in Florida in 1936. The Gaillacs, husband and wife, listen politely to the origins of Thanksgiving but with less fascination than might have been expected from the intellectually curious, especially with Gustave being a historian. Had they known it all already? Gustave admits that this is the first he has heard of Thanksgiving, confirming my suspicion that he never read the invitation. His speciality is the medieval Cathars or Albigensians of Languedoc. They were a heretical, ascetic

58

sect who banned sexual intercourse (also milk and cheese) but did not persecute those believers who failed to be perfect. By the fifteenth century they, the Cathars, had been wiped out by certain crusading popes and the Inquisition. Madame Gaillac says she gave up history seventeen years ago on the birth of her first child.

Having shaken hands with the guests, Kate and Polly rush from the room with the jigsaw, pursued by Gaillac teenagers. I tour again with the whiskey sours while the conversation splinters: the approaching elections for mayor and council, parking problems, prices. Where are the Foissacs and their small son, the student of judo? Already they are half an hour late. We are aiming to have dinner on the table at eight. Lucy, rising to the occasion, appears in jeans and a T-shirt bearing the Statue of Liberty in sequins. She shakes hands, answers questions about school, and fades from the room like ectoplasm the moment conversation reverts to Cahors politics.

The chef slips into the kitchen to put the spoon bread soufflé in the oven. The apéritif is going well. Marie-Claude lowers a tissue from in front of her nose to say she might try une larme, a tear. Madame Radiguet declines a second glass but Monsieur and Madame Gaillac, now smoking cheroots, progress with only minor protests from a second to a third. No nibbles, incidentally. The French seldom take snacks with apéritifs so we thought we wouldn't. There'll be enough to feed on once we get to the table. Apart from the missing Foissacs, Thanksgiving is cheerfully on course. Discussion takes in pedagogy, restaurants, the weather, and local personalities Catherine and I have never heard of. At eight-fifteen a pain racks my ribs. The chef is nudging me. 'How long,' she wants to know out of the side of her mouth, 'do we wait for the Foissacs? The soufflé's going to be ruined.'

We would telephone the Foissacs if we had a telephone. The conversation hops from Cahors politics to the Truffaut film at the Palais, then back to the mayoral elections. Marie-Claude thinks she might try another apéritif, for her cold. At nine o'clock the Foissacs arrive with a rush, apologetic and bearing a lavish gift of prunes in brandy for St Catherine's Day. The judo session had gone on and on because of the distribution of awards. Their son, aged nine, was awarded a yellow belt. The belt is passed round and admired. The son goes off with Kate and Polly to the jigsaw. The apéritif jug has to be replenished. Everyone talks at once.

For the Foissacs I try to emulate Catherine's account of the meaning of Thanksgiving, and acquit myself with exceptional fluency, in my view. Yet the Foissacs have difficulty in grasping even the basic facts of *les pellerons* – the Pilgrims. Monsieur looks baffled, and Madame astonished. What's so astonishing about the Pilgrims? Not only are the Foissacs unaccustomed to the strength of this Yankee apéritif but they are clearly overtired from the judo awards. 'À table!' Catherine calls. Still talking, the Foissacs muttering to each other, everyone files through the kitchen, a hall, a bedroom, and into Kate's bedroom, for tonight the dining-room. The French for pilgrim, I am to discover, is *pèlerin*. *Pelleron* is baker's peel, whatever that may be.

The room by candlelight with red paper tablecloths and two striped and starry flags over the chimney breast brings a burst of applause. Madame Radiguet seats herself at one end of the table in Gustave's place, removes his name card from her plate without looking at it, and spreads her napkin on her lap. This makes nonsense of the entire intricate logistics of who is to sit where, but by this stage neither host nor hostess is up to doing anything about it. The guests are sitting down where they choose, chattering without pause. What matters is that the children are at their own table. They are already seated, pouring lemonade and so starved that any moment now they will start rhythmically clattering their spoons as in a prison riot film. A start has been made on the Pont Valentré near the hearth and pieces of jigsaw puzzle lie scattered around.

The French serve vegetables and meat as separate courses. We serve the sprouts and chestnuts separately, combining as the main course the turkey, turkey sausages, and sweet and roast potatoes (Polly has insisted on roast potatoes, her favourite). The cranberry sauce is on the table at the start and at the end of the meal, untouched by most of the guests, who believe it to be jam for the equally strange soda bread, and an error, perhaps leftovers from breakfast. The soufflé, being in a dire condition, which is to say the consistency of rock, thanks to the Foissacs' arriving two hours late, is served only to those who ask, which is scarcely anyone as the entire room is talking so busily that our repeated requests for soufflé orders pass unheeded. The rest of the menu is discussed, eaten, praised, and with one possible exception, enjoyed.

Soupe de Tomate et Céleri

Choux de Bruxelles
et Châtaignes Mornay

Rôti de Dindonneau
Saucisses de Dinde
Pommes de Terre Rôties
Pommes de Terre Douces
Soufflé de Semoule de Maïs
Sauce aux Airelles

Vin nouveau de pays

Tarte aux Citrouilles
Tarte aux Fruits Secs

Café   Cognac

We begin with sufficient food for two rugby teams. Two hours later nothing remains except one of the four turkeys, the Impressionist flag, and most of the two pumpkin pies – the tarte aux citrouilles. Avid as the French are for pumpkin, usually as soup, they have never heard of pumpkin pie, and though everyone accepts a tiny sample, few come back for more. The dried fruit pie, also unknown to our guests, vanishes fast. The sprouts and chestnuts Mornay too are unfamiliar. So unfamiliar to Monsieur Foissac that both chef and commis notice him eyeing his portion speculatively, as if wondering whether this might be the baker's peel. At the tumultuous children's table we notice two Gaillac teenagers grimacing at each other as they sip undiluted lemonade.

We have little opportunity for noticing more. Two reasons why this dinner is hectic for the chef and commis are the number of guests and the dining-room being two rooms distant from the kitchen. French people at table don't generally wait until everyone is served before starting to eat, with the result that by the time Catherine and I are served and have rushed the food back to the oven to keep warm, Madame Radiguet, the Foissacs, and several Gaillacs are mopping their plates with bread and looking round for more.

Most of the serving is done from squatting positions in the umbrageous but relatively free area on the floor by the hearth. Some years down the line Catherine will tell me she retains two main memories of this Thanksgiving in Cahors. One, the curious molecular reaction that takes place when, crouched in the hearth, she pours gravy. Briskly the plate would curl at the edges and spout gravy to the floor. Two, the persistent roar of talk as children and teenagers, skidding in gravy and pieces of jigsaw, bring their misshapen plates for more.

Our guests give us no reason to suppose they are aware this is a frenetic evening for the chef and commis, which is as it should be. They are too busy talking, eating, and drinking. Even Marie-Claude with her cold succeeds in simultaneously talking and eating while holding a tissue to her nose. By the time coffee and brandy are circulating and host and hostess are ready to sit back and catch up on conversation, the hour is midnight and Madame Radiguet is looking at her watch.

The Foissac lad is asleep on the bed, holding his yellow belt. Lucy and the teen mob have long since departed to her room and rock records. Embracing, still chattering, leaving on the table the menu cards which they are supposed to take away as a souvenir, the guests heave on their coats.

Lafayette, as far as I'm aware, which admittedly isn't far, has not been mentioned. Good. He can be held in reserve for next Thanksgiving.

Next Thanksgiving? We plan to win the Irish Sweepstake so we may reserve a table at London's Connaught Hotel where they put on a knowledgeable Thanksgiving dinner, and presumably know their *pellerons* from their *pèlerins*.

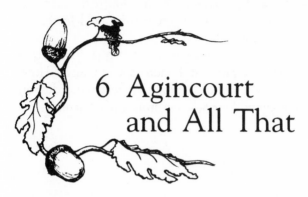

6 Agincourt and All That

S O WHO is this Gambetta, this grocer's son who has given his name to the main boulevard of Cahors? The name is about as French as Kate and Polly's Monsieur Spiaggi. In the Place Aristide Briand, which gives onto the boulevard, Gambetta's statue dominates as loftily as that of Queen Victoria in towns in Britain.

Léon Gambetta (1838–82), born in Cahors, was a politician and Republican leader of Genoese-Jewish lineage and progressive views. In 1870, after Napoleon III surrendered to the Prussians, he was one of the proclaimers of the Republic. With Paris under siege, he escaped in a balloon to rally the provinces and send armies against the invader, though to little avail. In the winter of 1881–82 Gambetta was premier of France, then he died from the effects of an accidental wound in the hand from a revolver. I don't know the details. I haven't seen his glass eye either, which, we are told, is in the town museum. I have toured the museum but failed to find the eye. Perhaps it is locked in a vault. The student standing in as curator the day I visited might as well have been selling lottery tickets for all he knew about the eye or anything else in the museum.

The Boulevard Gambetta is a stunning sight, though less so than before chrome and glass began to take over from mouldering stone. The broad avenue of shops and banks slopes down to the Pont Louis-Philippe over the Lot. Lining it are mottled plane trees, severely pollarded in the French fashion. An improvement fifteen years after we arrive in the rue Joffre, and not a minute too soon, will be the bypass that allows traffic to whizz across the hills rather than clog the boulevard. Not that rush-hour congestion won't persist in the 1990s. For whatever arcane reason too many cars, motor cycles, and behemoth lorries and tankers, prefer the Boulevard Gambetta to the bypass. To sit with a beer at a pavement table and watch the world and his wife go by, at peak time, is to be deafened and suffocated by the fuming traffic. Trucks bearing oil, sand, furniture, yogurt, blast past an arm's length away.

The sweetest peace is along the banks of the Lot, which loops in a horseshoe shape round the town. The best smells are in the alleys of the old quarter, if pungency is what you like: coffee, garlic, bread, Gauloise smoke from an old man on a chair in a doorway, cat, in summer a whiff of drains, and dubious odours from savaged garbage bags and upended pails put out too soon and discovered by dogs. Dogs tend to be either kenneled, or, at dinner at the home of French friends in the countryside, on their hind legs with one paw in your crotch, one on the table, and their nose in your plate. But in these ancient alleys are ambulatory dogs on missions. Watch where you step.

How ancient? Not Roman, though the Romans were here, bringing vines and leaving walls, bits of which are still to be seen. The Romans in Cahors, and the Gauls before them, worshipped Divona, a sacred spring on the other side of the river, close by the Pont Valentré. The spring is a chilly, slightly spooky spot with explanatory charts and depth measurements on the cliff face, and known as the Fontaine des Chartreux because Carthusian monks first piped water from it to the town. Without this spring there would have been no Divona Cadurcorum, later called Cadurca, and today, Cahors. Natives of Cahors are Cadurciens and Cadurciennes. The town still gets its drinking water from this spring.

These mullioned windows, stone coats of arms, and hulking wooden doors with iron studs, and on the walls plaques dating them from the Middle Ages, are in the vieille ville between the Boulevard Gambetta and the river. All authentic, naturally with a touch of restoration here and there. Anyone buying property in the medieval quarter and thinking of restoring it with glass and chrome, and plonking a satellite dish on the roof, will need to think again. The town fathers are vigilant in preserving old Cahors.

One good reason for the town's charm is that it has come down in the world since its golden era seven hundred years ago. Cahors in the thirteenth century was immensely prosperous, a magnet for Lombard financiers, Europe's first banking city. The Avignon Pope John XXII, born in Cahors in 1244, founder of Cahors University, might have had something to do with this. He was a financial wizard, lending out money at interest all over the Continent. Alarmed by reformers who claimed that Christ had renounced the use of all property, as well he might be, he denounced them as heretics. He was himself accused of heresy because of his views on the Beatific Vision, but he modified them the day before he died, full of years, his papal coffers brimming.

After Pope John XXII, the Hundred Years War, and Cahors was done for.

Cadurciens enjoy ribbing the Brits, us rosbifs, about that war. Crécy, Poitiers, the Black Prince, Agincourt. 'Once more unto the breach, dear friends, once more!' They can afford to, they won it, with help from the sorceress and saint, Joan of Arc. They finally rid themselves of us in 1453 after the battle of Castillon, a battle I had never heard of any more than the French have heard of Crécy, Poitiers, and Agincourt. Cahors saw plenty of action. We English kept attacking the town without ever capturing it. When the Treaty of Bretigny ceded Cahors to us in 1360, the townspeople took no notice. They refused to give up the town. 'Ah, la Guerre de Cent Ans!' today's Cadurciens remind any Brit they can buttonhole, mightily amused. When the English quit Quercy in the middle of the fifteenth century, Cahors was depopulated, ruined. But we had lost and we left.

66

More trouble for the town during the religious wars of the sixteenth century. Cahors had refused to give itself up to the English, now it showed the same disrespect to King Henry of Navarre. A couple of decades earlier in Cahors, the catholics had murdered the protestants. They weren't now about to bow to a protestant peasant from darkest Navarre. (Henry's cultured wife, Margaret of Valois, spoke of him as a peasant. If it wasn't this Henry it was his father, another Henry, who boasted that he took a bath every year – presumably whether he needed it or not.) So Henry, in 1580, led his army across the Pont Valentré and in five days of bloody street fighting which he thoroughly enjoyed, emerging 'all blood and power' (his words), he sacked the town and slaughtered its catholics. 'Un combat impitoyable' is how my guide book from the tourist office describes it. The timbered, turreted house where Henry may have lived for a few days after the carnage stands by the river, restored, a must on the town's tourist trail.

Had anyone other than Henry stayed there the house might have long since collapsed from neglect. Henry became France's best-loved king, Henry IV, the first Bourbon king, and apparently the third most written-about Frenchman after Napoleon and Louis XIV. He was the one who converted to catholicism to become king, which he did with the comment, 'Paris vaut bien la messe'. Paris is well worth a mass. He was a peerless leader, valorous, glamorous, unifier of the nation, restorer of peace, and wise in every respect except his love affairs, strings of them. Vive l'amour! (Henry's wife, Margaret, was equally adulterous and colourful. Alexander Dumas wrote a novel about her. France approvingly remembers her as a poet, memoirist – memoirs that are read today – and licentious.)

England's kings and queens have no equivalent for Henry IV. We would need to imagine a mix of King Alfred, who burnt the cakes, Harold, shot in the eye by an arrow in 1066, Elizabeth I ('I know I have the body of a weak and feeble woman, but I have the heart and stomach of a king'), and the Queen Mum. Henry IV died from two thrusts of an assassin's knife. The assassin was François Ravaillac, a fanatic whose punishment was to be torn to pieces by horses going in different directions. In history books all assassins are fanatics.

In 1751 Cahors lost its university, abolished by Louis XV so as to give Toulouse University a boost. The professors and pupils left Cahors. In the Revolution, when the ancient provinces were carved into *départements*, Cahors lost the southern, richest part of Quercy. A hundred years later it lost its wine, celebrated since Roman times, to an invasion of lice which destroyed the vines. Hence today's depopulated Lot. Who, who needed to earn a living, would stay?

Next question, how fare fair Lucy, Kate, and Polly?

Kate and Polly are to be promoted! In the New Year they will join regular classes stocked with real French children! Adieu, Monsieur Spiaggi! Adieu, *Bonjour, Maman. Bonjour, Paul. Bonjour, Maman. Bonjour, Martine* . . . Whether Monsieur Spiaggi and George Raft, the headmaster, believe Kate and Polly to be now sufficiently integrated, or whether they have been cowed by the opinion spread abroad by Catherine, with calm reasonableness, that the girls might do better in normal classes, and should never have had this experimental hi-tech, hands-on, state-of-the-art, audio-visual nonsense foisted on them in the first place, we shall never know. Their parents being delighted with the promotion, Kate and Polly are delighted, though wondering if Taufik too will graduate out of the integrating class. Perhaps the entire class of six is to graduate. Will Monsieur Spiaggi be left jobless?

He won't be the only one. As far as helping Kate and Polly with basic French goes, I am increasingly redundant. Weeks have passed since we sat at the kitchen table with picture books, objects, and vocabulary lists. 'Polly, your turn. Qu'est-ce-que c'est?' 'C'est un cuillère or an une cuillère. Dad, may we go now?' I still know words they don't, like *transatlantique*. They know not only words I don't know – they may not be able to spell them but they speak them – but they erupt with tirades (against, for example, the lukewarm school soup with stale, floating bread) that sound exquisitely French. Though I am lost, their French friends – Elsa, Hélène, Lucy's pal Mariette – understand. Should Kate and Polly become fluent in French, I shall always be able to remind them that it was I, at the kitchen table in the rue Joffre, who taught them. Perhaps not *taught* them exactly, but started them off.

Lucy's friend Mariette is two or three years older and very bright, though with no English, or none she is willing to speak. As she is incapable of slowing her French, my communication with her is restricted. Mariette recently passed her baccalauréat, the exam you must pass if you are to go on to college or do anything orthodox and salaried with your life. She has become a frequent visitor to the flat. After pleasantries about the weather she and Lucy repair to Lucy's room, its door closes, and walls, windows and crockery shudder from the impact of rock blastings.

Is Mariette a suitable amie is the question. She has long black hair and brown eyes but is very pallid, like the sultry existentialists I never met on my first visit to Paris in 1949, but ached to. She certainly is no jogger, or even much of a walker, and she smokes a lot, but most of the French do, especially the young. She does not shave her armpits. This too is all right, hairy armpits on a woman being socially acceptable in France, though on hot days Mariette does exude a bit of a whiff, especially if for whatever reason she has felt obliged to walk fast. She does not shave for health reasons, claiming that underarm hair is essential for conducting away from the armpits sweat that would otherwise seep into the bloodstream. Under each eye she has a pocket of shadow. Catherine says this may be make-up but I don't think she believes it. Gossips volunteer that Mariette has been seen in cafés with people who do drugs, not that this is to impute anything to Mariette.

The last time I ever see Mariette is not in the flat but on the Boulevard Gambetta one morning next spring. She is being driven along the boulevard in the back seat of a police car, looking straight ahead with her brown, beringed eyes.

Only once since frost and cold elbowed autumn aside have Catherine and I entered a café. Unless you are a cardplayer or an impoverished student, sitting inside is not the same as sitting outside, watching the free show. But a friend visiting from London is shocked that we are not sharing in French café life. Cahors is not Paris, we inform him. Cahors collapses early in the evening. As far as night life goes we might as well be in Chipping Sodbury. The Boulevard Gambetta becomes a ghost boulevard. Folk might venture to one of the three cinemas if a hustled film is showing, such as *Apocalypse Now*, but the majority prefer to sit at their own kitchen table watching television. To the best of our knowledge Cahors has no glittering café life where painters and writers discuss Lacan, Derrida and Barthes, and students hatch the new Utopia. 'Nonsense, be my guests,' says our misguided friend, a literary agent. At eight in the evening, heads bowed into the wind, we struggle along the boulevard to the largest, and in summer the liveliest café, the Tivoli, where a half metre of ham sandwich will be made up on demand, and alcohol, coffee, hot chocolate, and writing paper, are instantly available.

Two men stand with glasses at the bar. A card game is in progress, which is agreeably French, though the players are not the two solemn, middle-aged men of the Cézanne painting but youths slamming down winning cards from a height with bellows of triumph. They have to bellow to be heard. The only other customers are a desultory group watching a TV with the volume turned up as loud as it will go. After an armagnac and fifteen minutes we depart, having seen all that is to be seen, and defeated by the TV.

Cahors glitters. Lights come on in the pollarded trees, strings of stars twinkle across the boulevard. Beneath our windows loudspeakers blast out carols. Christmas is coming, the goose is getting fat, and not a currant or raisin is to be found. This is as bizarre as the sugar shortage that struck in September, jam-making time. Catherine is desperate. Currants and raisins are a requisite for Christmas pudding and mince pies. We try the posh shop in the rue Foch where they have everything. Not currants and raisins though. The proprietor fires off a shrug. 'C'est une grosse crise, Madame. Le port de Marseille est bloqué.'

The port of Marseilles is bloqué? What new madness is this? Bloqué with what? We have read no news for days, national or international. Bloqué by some nation's navy? An impenetrable mat of surplus Golden Delicious (O my Cox's Orange Pippins long ago!) bobbing on the briny, blocking Marseilles in some indefinable protest against or in support of subsidies or foreign imports?

The girls return from the last day of school with the lunchroom Menu de Noël. The teachers had champagne, Kate says. Everyone had turkey. Beetroot and saucisson for starters, creamed potatoes and fried rice, then the roast turkey, and finally bûche de Noël (Yule log) and chocolates.

'Brilliant!' Polly says.

'Except the bûche de Noël,' says Kate.

'Yuk,' agrees Polly.

We commiserate, having bought from a pâtisserie a bûche de Noël during an earlier Christmas. Those there must be who enjoy this glorified Swiss roll, France's traditional Christmas dessert, but it is tooth-achingly sweet. Find the right cake shop and no doubt the bûche de Noël could be fine, but pastry chefs don't cut off a corner of this iced, frosted, chocolate-speckled, designer log for sampling in the way cheesemongers do.

We drive to the locked-up, closed-down holiday house at Catus where four months ago the crickets creaked their monotone and the wasps gate-crashed on the melon.

Bleakness, abandonment, the ground cracked by frost. Furtively, like robbers, which is what we are, we prowl into our former landlord's woods. We look about, select, and saw down one of the thousand junipers. Put another way, we purloin a Christmas tree, or what will pass as a Christmas tree.

The landlord in farthest Cambridgeshire will never know. No one will know. We are doing the environment and the landlord a favour by thinning out his woods, if only by one tree. The woods are not lovely but they are dark and deep, and so overgrown that the sun cannot penetrate. The trees are stunted and unhappy. If we had a telephone we would call Cambridgeshire and the landlord would say, 'Take all the trees you can carry so the sun may penetrate, rain may water the roots, and the woods flourish as they did in the days of our ancestors!' He owes us at least a tree for our having looked after his house that winter.

In the rue Joffre the girls festoon the tree with sculpted pastry stars and moons, painted and threaded egg shells, and garlands of homemade marshmallows and peppermint creams. Across the length of a baker's window we see JOYEUX NOËL spelled out in bread. A burly fellow arrives at the flat to give us a calendar, not one we would have chosen ourselves but no household can have too many calendars. He says he is a pompier, a fireman, and the calendar is free but if we would like to make a contribution? We scramble for francs. In London we never tipped firemen, we never met any, but here you do and I'm in favour of it. We are not sure if we are expected to tip the postman but we risk it and he is not insulted. We do not tip the dustmen. We would if ever we saw them but we only hear them. They come and go before anybody is awake. Back in Fulham, omit to give Mr Doolittle and his team a tip and you're likely to find your dust all over your front path.

Catherine makes plum puddings and mince pies, improvising, in lieu of currants and raisins, with dried apples, apricots, and prunes. Tomorrow, Christmas Eve, seven o'clock, we have invited twenty-five friends to drop by for potato soup, tuna salad, cheese, mince pies, and mulled wine. Nothing elaborate, no Thanksgiving this.

Whence cometh these twenty-five, should they happen by? The Thanksgiving mob. Elizabeth and Jean, the Anglo-French marriage, and their brood. Several of the rest seem to be teachers of English. Sylvette, who teaches at the catholic school; Pierre and Francine, married, both teaching English; another Pierre who teaches English, married to an Englishwoman. I am not averse to the company of these teachers whose English is superior to most English people's, and who, to boot, speak accentless French. Françoise, toiler in the chamber of commerce, speaks excellent English, having lived in Edinburgh. We have met her because Polly has made friends with her daughter, Elsa, a lithe and beautiful gymnast. The father is a brooding, bearded Spaniard, Gimi, who plays chess and the guitar, gives language lessons, and looks like an El Greco portrait of a conquistador.

To be ahead of the game, Catherine makes her smashing Irish soda bread on the eve of Christmas Eve. Also a creamy, foolproof potato soup, leaving the tureen on the floor by the stove. Next morning when we lift the lid the soup is bubbling. Is it turning into vodka? We tip the soup down the sink. The stove dies, as it tends to do when we need it. Increasingly foul-tempered, sooty-faced, piling in more and more kindling, charcoal, and firelighters, three times I fail to get the stove going, the coal being resolutely fireproof. Catherine recalls that ovens must be relit with new, unused coal. I'm in no mood for folklore from the bogs of Ireland. New, unused coal brought by leprechauns wearing green smocks and shamrocks, right? After she has marched out wordlessly for potatoes I reset the oven with new, unused coal, and it works.

The first guests, teachers, arrive dismayingly early at six, bringing flowers. They apologize but they can stay only a moment, they must meet parents at the railway station, but joyeux Noël, and all right, a very quick . . . what is it again?

Mince pie? They have never met mincemeat. They follow their slice of mince pie with a second, and to help it along Monsieur takes a second glass of vin chaud. He's familiar with mulled wine, requests the recipe, embraces the next arrivals, encourages them not to hold back on the mulled wine and mince pie, and is led away by Madame fifteen minutes after Madame's parents' train is due at the station.

Guests arrive with more hothouse flowers, chocolates, a duck pâté, a bûche de Noël. 'Pour les huîtres!' exclaims Gustave Gaillac, extending two bottles of Alsatian white wine. For the oysters. That explains the countless crates of variously graded oysters in the market. Oysters and white wine are evidently a Christmas custom. Françoise brings a Spanish omelette packed with onion and potato. Everyone has a slice except her husband, the bearded Gimi. 'Sangría!' he cries, like an oath, after his first sip of mulled wine, and thereafter occupies himself exclusively with the hot wine and yearnings for his homeland. I make more mulled wine, then more again, sloshing new wine and unmeasured spices into the remnants of the old, and heating and stirring. The concoction bears less and less resemblance to the original.

Shortly before midnight we descend into the empty street with our last guests, Gimi and Françoise. Even the Boulevard Gambetta is deserted. 'Look, no one!' Gimi exclaims with a wave of his arm. 'The French are not sociable! In Spain people are strolling up and down until three, four in the morning!'

In Cahors many of the townsfolk are in the cathedral awaiting midnight mass. We find standing room. 'Ave Mari-i-a,' sings the congregation.

Back in the flat we clear up. We put the filled Christmas stockings at the end of the girls' beds. How old do they have to be before they will no longer demand a stocking?

7 Noël

THE FIRST problem on Christmas Day for the girls is deciding where they will hoard their Christmas money. They stroke it and hold it up to the light like speculators on a winning streak, but it will be gone before the January sales if a decision isn't made quickly. These crinklies are not for frittering but for knee-high leather boots, à la mode in Cahors this year. The decision is to hand the money to Dad, mistakenly considered a safe bet. Before the week is out the cash is swallowed up in housekeeping, and I am in debt by three pairs of boots.

Second dire problem, should the goose and plum pudding be for lunch or supper? We have been invited to the home of Madame Radiguet, the aristocratic widow with the marriageable daughter, to meet others of her family and have a little something to eat. What sort of hour is five, what will the eats be, and what quantity? If we have the goose for lunch we'll hardly be ready to plant our feet in the trough again at five. If we have a biscotte for lunch, and Madame Radiguet's little something turns out to be a bowl of cashews, we shall faint from hunger. The girls vote for lunchtime goose. Seize the hour, gather ye rosebuds.

Accompanying the goose and improvised plum pudding are toasts to absent friends, which widen to include absent acquaintances, Kate and Polly becoming so carried away that soon we are toasting the postman, various invented people, and the terrapins, Cherubim and Seraphim. Here the girls are limited as to pets, not least because of the quarantine laws on returning to Britain, which we might, and we might not; no decision has been made and we don't much think about it. Lucy seems to have advanced beyond pets, but for Kate and Polly terrapins seem to be an adequate solution. I say they are boring, but Catherine awards them ten out of ten for precisely that reason. They don't have to be put out and whistled in as does our London cat; they don't create a night-long racket as did the hamsters, nor keep being discovered belly-up as did the goldfish, or eat the postage-stamp of a lawn down to the roots as did the guinea pigs.

From England has arrived a board game named The Magnificent Race which passes the afternoon. Catherine and I are happy to leave board games to board-game freaks, but The Magnificent Race has a novel aspect, a spinning roulette-type wheel into which you tip coloured balls, and out of which they can fly and strike you in the eye, keeping the players alert, not to say on edge. And so to five o'clock.

Madame Radiguet greets us wan of face and wearing a headband, like a tennis player at Wimbledon. Additional scarves envelop her neck. Not only has she a cold, she says in a faraway voice, but she is suffering from gueule de bois. I know the expression, 'Ta gueule!' (Shut your gob), but gueule de bois is new to me. I draw Lucy aside. 'Literally, a wooden throat,' Lucy explains. 'In effect, a hangover.' After midnight mass Madame evidently attended a one o'clock Christmas breakfast of champagne, oysters, black pudding, and hot chocolate. Sympathy for her gueule de bois therefore eludes me, though I am happy to know the expression. Coming to grips with the customs of France, the epicurean flights, to say nothing of party hours, is not easy.

For two hours guests arrive, nibble on potato crisps, and sip hot infusions of hyssop and lemon verbena, or alcohol. We meet a son who promotes La Vache Qui Rit, the packaged triangles of processed cheese (which I like), and a daughter just back from a holiday in Cuba. Madame Radiguet is not a widow, as it turns out. She has a husband, or former husband, living in Africa, an ex-diplomat she hasn't seen for twenty years. The children have disappeared to the TV for circuses and Charlot – Charlie Chaplin. The only foreign comedian to compete in popularity with Charlot is Jerry Lewis, Légion d'honneur.

(Woody Allen? France's cinema intelligentsia believes that France alone, i.e. themselves, truly loves and understands Woody Allen. Certainly Americans don't, with the possible exception of enclaves of Jewish intellectuals in Brooklyn. They are so serious about him you wonder if he ever actually makes them, the intelligentsia, laugh. The *Le Monde* review of *Shadows and Fog*, February 13, 1992, goes on about 'spatial continuum', 'cosmopolitan construct', and 'the unbelievable power of Allen's direction [that] enables characters to transcend their purpose in life and become universal archetypes.')

At seven the party drifts into the dining-room for the little something to eat. This proves to be not too gargantuan, a champagne buffet kicking off with chicken consommé and progressing through smoked ham, duck pâté, a ballotine of cold pressed chicken in aspic, and salad. Then cheese, our regional Cabécou and Cantal plus impressive Roquefort for cheese connoisseurs. Next bought cakes and tarts, and a pumpkin pudding. Why deny it, the pumpkin pudding is bland by comparison with Catherine's pumpkin pies.

Amid popping champagne corks, our scarf-swathed hostess palely but gamely attentive, Christmas Day winds to a close, and none too soon. Other invitations lie ahead. Of friends we ask in to help with leftovers let it merely be recorded that the plum pudding and brandy butter vanish like smoke, one customer mopping with bread the last pudding crumbs and smears of brandy butter on his plate.

On Boxing Day we see Lucy off on a school bus for five days' skiing in the Pyrenees. Then we drive into the frosty hills for lunch at the weekend retreat of Pierre, a tax inspector.

He's the third or fourth Pierre we've come to know. In Wales he would be Pierre the Tax to distinguish him from Pierre the Teacher, Pierre the Bald Teacher, and so on, our other Pierres all being teachers, but at our first meeting, before we learned his occupation, he asked in a hushed voice, 'Êtes-vous croyant?' Are you a believer? He is, he lets us know in a spooky whisper as if in church. We guessed he meant he was a keen Roman Catholic, but he didn't enlarge, dropping the subject after I replied that I had been sent to Quaker schools. So anyway to us he is Pierre the Believer, or Spooky Pierre, and with him is his son, about to enter medical college, who dominates the conversation with success stories in the field of alternative medicine: homeopathy, hypnotism, faith-healing, biofeedback, massage, maggot therapy, crystals, sweat baths. I am tempted to suggest he keep quiet about this at medical college, at least until he has passed his first exams, but any comment at all will keep him talking, and I'm getting hungry. Where's lunch?

For miles on all sides unrolls a panorama of forsaken, white-dappled hills, and for two hours sunshine warms the air. Father and son are proud of the view, the cottage, and the old stone bakehouse with working oven. Herein, on a table, are a square yard of uncooked pizza topped with rows of Gruyère, sausage, mushrooms, anchovies, and olives, and an apple tart of the same dimension. Like a scene in a Brueghel painting, the son fuels the oven and rakes the embers to achieve an even temperature. 'We don't often use this oven,' Pierre says. 'It's the business of collecting enough wood.' The son seizes a pole and slides the pizza then the tart into the oven. They are using it in our honour.

We sit in the sun with a bottle of Cahors wine. When the chefs return to the bakehouse and peek into the oven to check on progress, they find an inferno. Half the pizza is burned black, its edge in flames. Some time later, dessert time, the apple tart is found to be soggily half cooked and has to be returned to the failing warmth of the oven. The coffee is thin. We are fulsome in our thanks but must rush because our daughters await us, they have an engagement, we must chauffeur them. The girls are always an unimpeachable excuse for flight.

The following day snow falls then thaws into slush. In the night comes a heavy frost, and when we drive into the country for another lunch the landscape is tinselly white, the hills, bare trees, vineyards of stumpy vines, and tiled roofs of farmhouses all covered with frost.

During introductions and handshakings a well-tailored Frenchman, in one flowing movement like a dance step, takes a pace forward, lifts and kisses Catherine's hand, and steps back. The deed is done so deftly, with such absence of affectation, I can only goggle and admire. The kiss is pure cinema, the bloke must be a resting actor from the Comédie Française. Catherine accepts the compliment without blinking, though it's not every day she has her hand professionally kissed so far as I know. The well-tailored man is a count, our hostess tells us in a murmured aside. We understand that this is sufficient explanation for his gallantry.

On New Year's Eve (in the baker's window the sculpted bread spells out BONNE ANNÉE) my turn comes. I am kissed by assorted Frenchmen, not on the hand, but, like` a Mafia victim, on both freshly-shaved, cologne-splashed cheeks. True, New Year's Eve is exceptional, but we feel we have arrived, the two of us, kissed into la vie Lotoise. (The girls, as children, are continually kissed, and though at first fed up about it, now accept it.) New Year's Eve is with a party of twenty at the house of a Cahors academic and his midwife wife. The scene is from a movie of party life among the beautiful people: doctors, lawyers and professors of both sexes in a setting of flickering firelight, abstract paintings, and leather upholstery.

Christmas in France is for family, New Year's Eve is for friends. Most of the people here we have never met but we are made welcome. The apéritif is kir made from blackcurrant juice and a sparkling white Burgundy. We seat ourselves round several tables pushed together and covered with a white linen tablecloth, and start the first course – each couple has brought a course – the prince of all Lot specialities, foie gras. Hardly has the foie gras been demolished when a blast of rock music issues from an adjoining salon and the assembly rises and files through to dance.

Dancing continues for twenty minutes until, abruptly, the music is switched off and everyone returns to the dining-room for lobster tails, tomatoes, and mayonnaise. Then more dancing. And so on through the evening, the champagne corks popping, and our host remembering every so often to toss another log on the fire. Midnight strikes towards the end of the turkey-and-chestnut-stuffing course, and it is now that everyone rises and circles the table in random directions, kissing and wishing each other a bonne année. Everyone, that is, except Catherine, fidgeting with her turkey (not her favourite meat), abstracted, and somewhat disbelieving of the circling and kissing. She'll rise in a moment or two, after making a decision on the turkey, but meanwhile, because she remains seated, everyone has to come to kiss her, and wish her bonne année, so her turkey grows yet colder as she lifts her face this way and that for kisses.

There follows dancing, endive salad, dancing, the little circular goat cheese of Quercy known as Cabécou, more dancing, gâteaux and glaces, dancing, Cognac, more champagne, and dancing, though with longer passages of time slumped in the armchairs round the fire.

And now, please God, may we return to routine, school, work, and more frugal living?

This winter is mildish for the most part: paltry snow and no frozen pipes. Cahors is calm and grey. The town's single highest money-spinner, tourism, is on hold until spring. Posters for local elections are being pasted on walls but civic enthusiasm is muted. Gustave, our helpful politician with the bad back and five children, is out and about, politicking. Madame Radiguet, on the other hand, considers election time in Cahors a proper occasion for visiting her sister in Paris for two months. We drive her to the railway station.

Lucy, lightly-bronzed from skiing, has scored eighteen out of twenty for her French essay, which mark, she reminds us, is genius level. All grading is out of twenty and marks tend to be miserly. Nine and ten out of twenty isn't at all bad. Twelve is on the way to brilliance and awarded grudgingly. For her Latin, Caesar still and for ever moving into winter quarters, Lucy receives four. Kate and Polly, now in separate, normal classes of a score or more French ruffians, are speaking, gabbling even, what sounds remarkably like French. But speaking and writing are chevaux of a different colour. We sense that Kate, in a more advanced class than Polly because she is older, may be floundering. She returns home one evening thoughtfully. In French dictation she spelled only one word correctly. Years later she will confess she floundered in spades. 'I wrote every word as I heard it, phonetically. I wrote gobbledygook.'

Is facility in foreign languages a gift, a matter of an attentive ear, or of grinding application? (I recall reading how the historian A.J.P. Taylor, as a student, was told airily by his tutor, 'Anyone can read Italian.') Catherine, resolved to become fluent, as in time she will be, works at her French, taking every opportunity to speak and read it. She would like us to speak it among ourselves, as the Strides sometimes do, but I become self-conscious and feel under siege. Top of my list of disadvantages to the expatriate life in France is the language. I can't understand why this doesn't seem to bother other Brits living here. Their French sounds to me no better than mine. Jim Wolfe, for example, the retired gentleman living some miles away along the twisty road, speaks good French but with such care and slowness that you want to finish his sentences for him, in French or English.

Not that I'm not improving. I have learned to hail people with 'Salut!' (Salute!), rather than 'Salaud!' (Whore!). For half a dozen swift sentences, buying onions, tossing in a comment on the weather, exclaiming 'Alors!' and 'Eh voilà!' with the appropriate gesture learned from all those old Raimu and Fernandel films, I pass muster. I have been asked if I am Dutch, and Alsatian, though remain in the dark as to whether I should feel encouraged or dismayed.

What if you do more than pass muster? What if your few clichés are so convincingly, flamboyantly French that you are taken to be fluent, and the person you're with jabbers on impenetrably like a chipmunk on a scrambled telephone? Naturally, you ask him to slow down please, you're not that proficient, yes? It is not so simple. He won't believe you, or he doesn't hear, and he continues his unfathomable discourse. I have become expert in reacting with gestures, snorts, and sighs, which lead whoever has me cornered to believe I am drinking in his every word. How do I know when to snort and when to sigh? From the tone of his voice and by watching his eyes. Or her eyes. Conversation by reaction is not difficult. You need to be alert and a bit of a ham. After five minutes of an exchange in which I neither understand nor utter a word, but nod and agree a great deal, we shake hands and go our ways, if in the street, or someone else will pick up the conversation, if at table, allowing me a respite from gesturing and snorting.

Ah, but if he interrupts his flow with what you believe, horrified, must be a direct question arising from the topic, because he stops speaking and looks you in the eyes, awaiting an answer, what then? Here the game gets dodgier but it is by no means lost. You do as before – 'Mais . . .!' and 'Eh . . .!' and 'Alors . . .!' – but so gripped by the question that you cannot for the moment find the right words. Your sputtering and exclaiming correctly evoke delight, disgust, dismay, whatever the particular passion his tone has been conveying, and if you stand steadfast, sooner rather than later he will shout the answer for you. Now is the moment to slap your sides and cry, 'Mais oui! Voilà! C'est comme ça! Au revoir! Enchanté! A la prochaine!' Such fluency confirms his belief that he has enjoyed an intelligent and entertaining conversation.

Linguistic pitfalls abound. At supper at the home of Raymond and Ginette, tamperers with identity cards, I decline a third helping, saying, 'Merci, je suis plein.' Eyebrows hike up. Merci, je suis plein, it transpires, means, Thank you, I am pregnant. After this I should have shut up, but the local red shunts the language along wondrously, and in full sail I hear myself praising France's military heroes. Charlemagne, Joan of Arc, Napoleon, Brigadier-General Christian Marie Ferdinand de la Croix de Castries, commander at Dien Bien Phu. Eyebrows crush against the hairline. Too late, it turns out that an s does not elide with a silent h. Spoken, les halles – the covered market – becomes lay alle, not lez alle. Les héros becomes lay ero, not lez ero, as I am saying it. Lez ero to a French listener is les zéros, the nothings. I am impressing on the company that their greatest soldiers are nothings.

The worst curse is vous and tu. You, gentle reader with excellent French, will not need reminding, but for those who may like their memory nudged, vous is the formal 'you', tu is for family, close friends, children, and animals. To commit the solecism of addressing the wrong person as tu, someone you are not intimate with, be it the President of the Republic or the baker's wife who sells you your daily bread, is to offend them mightily. Catherine will return to the flat aghast and suicidal. 'I bumped into Madame Dupont, we chatted, and I staggered into tu! I retreated into vous but she'd noticed!' The line between vous and tu, usually obvious enough, can be paper thin. 'You go with your feeling,' Lucy explains. This is correct but not invariably helpful. What is less reliable than feeling? Not that it is any great consolation but the French too err. We hear confessions of jolly evenings – 'Chevaliers de la table ro-c-onde, Goûtons vo-o-oir si le vin est bon!' – where unabashed tutoying results in the offender awaking from nightmares mortified by the impertinence. Vous versus tu being tricky for the French, for Brits it's a minefield, though as foreigners we may be forgiven on grounds of ignorance.

Maybe but not necessarily. Which form you choose to use, what you get away with, what you permit others to get away with, derives from a mishmash of savoir-faire, experience, upbringing, going with your feeling, and, I suspect, politics. Raymond and Ginette, on the right, address us as vous, and for us to address them as tu would be a gaffe perhaps rendering the friendship kaput. Gustave, left-wing politician, hustles about shaking hands and tutoying everybody.

For myself, vous or tu is no longer a problem. Forget tu. Vous for everyone. Vous for the dogs in the street. I am in distinguished company. I have read that President de Gaulle addressed his wife as vous. We shouldn't believe everything we read, but this could be true, De Gaulle having been a law unto himself.

We are not yet done with seasonal customs. On Twelfth Night – le Jour des Rois – in bakers' shops and cake shops, appears the Epiphany galette, a round sweet loaf of bread which keeps reappearing until the end of January.

Each galette comes with a cardboard crown, and inside each galette is a bean. Whoever receives the slice of galette containing the bean is king, or queen, and wears the crown. The drawback to this otherwise harmless custom is that whoever wears the crown must also buy galettes for the rest of the company. So if you win, you lose, as with the golfers' custom of standing drinks all round after a hole in one. On the last day of the month and of the galette season Catherine returns dazed from helping officiate at her school lunch. As well as conducting conversation classes she now supervises infants in a school dining-room, tying on their bibs, helping them cut their rôti de porc, and generally looking after them during the two-and-a-half hours between morning and afternoon school. 'The din was shattering,' she complains.

'I sympathize. All those children.'

'Not the children at all, it's the teachers!' says she, indignant. 'They had champagne and those dreadful galettes and were wearing crowns and you never heard such an uproar.'

Thus proliferates the sale of galettes. 'C'est le commerce,' sceptical Monsieur Foissac will surely growl should we meet him, but we don't.

But I do bump into another friend from Catus days, Monsieur Becquet, farmer. He extends an invitation. Something to do with truffles, I think. If only he would speak more slowly . . .

8 Here We Come a-Truffling

MONSIEUR BECQUET is walking from the covered market, a square weatherbeaten figure in overcoat and beret on a rare visit to the metropolis, Cahors. On his boots is a dusting of snow. We shake hands.

'Bonjour, M'sieu' Kenyon.' He pronounces it Kng-yng in a shout. The English are not the only nation to shout in order to be understood by foreigners. 'Voulez-vous chercher des truffes?'

I would indeed like to hunt for truffles. Perhaps only once, but once certainly. When and where?

'Chez moi. Deux heures, demain?'

Demain he pronounces demeng in the accent of the south-west and of the Midi generally. A remark such as, 'So, my friends, now is the end', emerges as 'Enfeng, mes copengs, mainteneng c'est le feng'.

'Demain, deux heures, merci,' I say, and we shake hands again, grinning at one another in bewildered expectation.

'Bieng! A demeng, M'sieu' KNG-YNG!'

I sprint to the flat and *Larousse Gastronomique* for homework on truffles. An outsider, eavesdropping, might be excused for supposing the people of the Lot talk at times of little else. I spied truffles in the market last Saturday, ugly, black, wrinkled things in closely-guarded baskets, not unlike prunes only bigger, hard, dry, and smelly. They are considered ambrosial. One recent winter during a bountiful truffle harvest, the boxed truffles stacked at Cahors railway station awaiting the train to Paris, residents in the area complained of the smell. Off to the station sped the town sanitation department to spray it with air-freshener.

My only other knowledge of truffles, this side of *Larousse Gastronomique*, is that they are pricey, costing I don't know, several gold ducats per gram. As when buying a yacht, if you need to ask the price you can't afford them. Choose a truffled item on the menu and you can double the price of the same item untruffled. To these truffles in the market adheres a hint of earth as evidence of authenticity and freshness, but only a hint. They are sold by weight, weighed meticulously, and nobody is going to pay for adhering carbuncles of soil.

'TRUFFLE. Truffe – Subterranean fungus of which a number of varieties exist. The black truffle of Périgord and that of the Lot are the most highly esteemed. Truffles are also gathered in Dauphiné, Burgundy and Normandy and in various other regions in France, but all these are inferior in quality and have a less delicate aroma.'

That's about all *Larousse Gastronomique* has to say, apart from there being a white, garlic-flavoured truffle in North Italy; the truffle's food value is problematical, white or black; a truffle's close texture makes it difficult to digest; and two pages of recipes. Truffles stewed in butter and cream, truffles cooked in champagne or Madeira, truffle fritters, truffle soufflés, truffle rissoles.

My mother made smashing rissoles without truffles. I doubt she'd heard of truffles, other than the chocolate ones. She would grind up Sunday's leftover roast of beef – usually it would be Tuesday before the leftovers reached this final stage – by turning the handle of a friendly iron grinder which she clamped to the edge of the kitchen table. Add onion, a dash of Worcestershire for daring, massage into rissole shapes, and Bob's your uncle, as the saying went. Heat in a pan and serve with spuds and cabbage. The rissoles would be overcooked (by French standards the original Sunday roast had been overcooked), grey, and delicious. They were at their pinnacle of deliciousness when accidentally burnt, especially those charred, crunchy bits which fell away from the rissole and sizzled in the bottom of the pan. The addition of a truffle would have ruined the rissole for us, I'm sure of it. Confronted with any of the recipes in *Larousse Gastronomique* my mother would have gone blank, as would we all. Sauté of truffles Brillat-Savarin, for example. Brillat-Savarin was the know-all who said, 'Tell me what you eat and I will tell you what you are.' Here is what he proposes we do. 'Peel 12 large truffles' – There goes a month's salary for a start – 'which must be perfectly ripe, black, firm and regular. Cut each into four or five thick slices. Season with salt, freshly ground pepper and spice. Just a few minutes before serving, sauté the truffles in quail fat, taking care not to fry them. Drain them and set them in a low crust of puff pastry. Dilute the cooking juices with Madeira, add a little concentrated veal stock, cook down and pour over the truffles.'

Another source book offers under Truffle: '. . . refuses to be cultivated . . . often grows a foot deep, normally under oak trees but also under birch, willow, elm, and aspen . . . Not easy to find . . . traditionally hunted by pigs, usually young sows . . . Can appear sliced in salads, stuffings, pâté de foie gras, or whole and raw, dipped in brandy, or cooked in the ashes of a fire . . . The "black diamonds" of Périgord . . . popular since the 15th century . . . reputed aphrodisiac qualities . . .'

Never mind aphrodisiac qualities, what about us truffle hunters, do we need to bring special equipment when going truffling? I mean you don't go fishing without a fishing rod. Protective clothing, gloves, respirator? Monsieur Becquet may have advised on this and I missed it. Big boots for warding off the pig? Who knows how frisky or hostile it might be? Monsieur Becquet will presumably supply the pig. Scales and calculator to measure our progress towards millionairedom?

Monsieur Becquet's millionairedom, that is. I shall be present as an impartial observer.

Here we come a-truffling
   Among the woods and dales;
Here we come a-truffling
   With ledger and with scales;
Love and joy from on high!
Lead us where the truffles lie!
   Just make note that for Brillat-
   Savarin, use quail fat,
Then sauté, sauté, sauté –
Do not fry!

Two o'clock chez Monsieur Becquet's farm, and here comes
Monsieur in working blues, jerseys, muffler, beret. Equipment
looks to be a basket, a tin can, and not a pig but a dog. Rin
Tin Tin.

'Bonjour, M'sieu' KNG-YNG! Ça va bieng? Fait froid, engh?'

A watery, February sun shines, melting the snow to slush.
For a kilometre we bucket and splash in Monsieur Becquet's
van along the lane, the three of us. Monsieur Becquet, moi,
and Monsieur's truffle hound, whose name is Diane. Truffle
dogs are often named Diane after the Roman goddess of the
moon, forests, and hunting, Monsieur Becquet says.

We park and debouch into scrofulous woodland. Sparse,
stunted oaks with bark blotched by green, tinselly stuff.
Underfoot is moss, soggy leaves, and snow where the sun
has failed to find its way.

'Diane, cherche!' commands Monsieur Becquet.

Diane bounds forward a metre or two, stops, and scrabbles
with her front paws at leaf mould and moss. Monsieur
Becquet smiles a knowing smile and advances. Calling to
Diane to stop, he stoops over the scrabbled earth and himself
scrabbles. He scrabbles more, more still, then straightens,
empty-handed. He gives Diane a sideways look, shrugs, and
mumbles that sometimes, not often but sometimes, Diane is
mistaken.

'Cherche, cherche!'

Diane bounds another metre, halts, and scrabbles. She is
a medium-size, medium-looking, grey-brown mongrel, wet-
nosed, lean, bouncy, and unabashed by her feeble beginning.

Again from Monsieur Becquet comes the command to desist. 'Arrête!' He scrabbles where Diane scrabbled and rises with a lump of golf ball sized mud in his hand. He sniffs it and offers it for sniffing. It smells of mud.

'C'est une truffe,' Monsieur Becquet says.

'Mon Dieu,' say I.

Monsieur Becquet dips into the tin can, brings forth a croûton, and tosses it to Diane, who gobbles it. This crusty cube of bread, perhaps baked in goose fat, who knows, is her reward. Monsieur flicks mud off the golf ball to reveal something wrinkled and warty under the mud.

'Cherche, Diane!'

Gallop, scramble, another soily ball. After ten minutes half a dozen balls of soil are in the bottom of the basket. Is it that I think I ought to be smelling something or do I in fact smell a peculiar scented something emanating from the basket? Yes, I do, an aromatic, piquant, truffle scent, the flavour you pay through the nose for when ordering truffled duck.

Smart dog, I remark. Smart as paint, agrees Monsieur, and he tosses Diane a croûton.

One of the reference books had observed, though remaining cautiously uncommitted, that the dogs credited with the keenest sense of smell are Spaniels, Poodles, and Pomeranians Monsieur Becquet says that truffle dogs smell acutely, are always smart, and are usually mongrels. They have to be trained. Their life expectation isn't long, only seven or eight years, hélas. The sniffing for truffles wears them out, he says.

Dead from sniffing out truffles? Here is a myth of rural France if ever I heard one. But Monsieur is serious. He gives the shrug, sad and accepting. He should know. Truffle hounds die young. C'est la vie. He tosses a bonus croûton to Diane.

His brother, the village postman, arrives in his yellow post office van. He wears a cloth cap and smokes a Gitane the colour of his van. We follow a path to a plot of land owned by the brother. 'Cherche, Diane!' he commands. Diane frisks forward, disinters a truffle, and is paid by the postman with a gobbet of meat. After half an hour Diane has sniffed out every truffle, about half a kilo's worth. Not great shakes, evidently, not like it used to be.

We cross the road into more woods where a Simca and its two occupants await us like mobsters in a getaway car. They are a woman and an unrelated retired Monsieur in a beret like a charred pancake who own patches of land on this side of the lane. Now, by appointment, Diane will hunt for them.

This she does more fruitfully than on her master's brother's patch, some of the retired Monsieur's truffles approaching tennis ball size. At the end of a further half hour, all truffles located and gathered, Monsieur is in possession of three kilos, which he carries in a striped football stocking. He quotes the price they will fetch in Cahors market on Saturday. Because of his breakneck patois I fail to grasp the figure, but if I had I'd have been little wiser. More than a decade after the introduction of the new franc, the older generation in the Lot still talk in terms of the old franc, worth a hundred times less than the new.

The afternoon is chilly. Drips form on noses. Diane sits panting, thumping her tail. In French larded with local slang the retired Monsieur narrates a tale the drift of which seems to be that a fish-eating Breton, stopping off at one of the two restaurants in the village, and being served truffled turkey, carefully set on the edge of his plate each bit of nasty black stuff in the belief that the restaurateurs of the Lot were out to poison him and steal his purse.

We climb a stone wall and head towards the lady's truffle patch. Not all dogs have a nose for truffles, Monsieur Becquet says, and those that have need training. In olden times pigs were used but you had to watch pigs because they ate the truffles. Truffle dogs aren't interested in eating truffles. They don't care for them. They're not gourmets but gourmands. They nose out truffles because of the reward after each nosing of a croûton or a scrap of meat. He offers Diane a truffle. She sniffs it and turns away.

91

Monsieur Becquet says truffle oaks are generally planted and his brother's are about finished, having been planted thirty years ago. The retired Monsieur's are younger, giving more and bigger truffles, and the bigger the truffle the better. Truffles are a winter crop, growing from about mid-December to the end of February, and in this period they can be hunted every eight days or so. He'll be hunting again next week. Madame Becquet conserves her truffles in eau-de-vie. His brother and the retired Monsieur sell theirs in Cahors.

Rain in late summer results in the best truffles, Monsieur Becquet says, warming to the job of edifying the Englishman. The poorest crop he remembers was in 1950 after a summer of drought. Sometimes one unearths a bad truffle, mushy inside, because winter came too soon and the snow has got to it. There have to be truffle oaks or a few other species of tree. But if there is a truffle oak that's no guarantee truffles will be found under it. On a sunny day a farmer with good eyesight can find truffles on his own, without a truffle dog, because flies swarm over the spot where the truffles lie buried. But the farmer can't generally smell them out. If they are there at all they are rarely more than three inches down.

I' refrain from mentioning that the book had said truffles often grow a foot deep. Perhaps those were Périgord truffles. This afternoon, in the Lot, they are invariably just below the soil's surface. Monsieur Becquet takes out a penknife and cuts into a truffle. It slices like Cheddar. The black inside is veined like a diagram in an anatomy book.

'Vas-y, cherche!'

Diane hunts on behalf of the woman who arrived with the retired Monsieur. The sun has gone, leaving the sky the colour of the postman's Gitane ash. Busy, eager, unfailingly obedient, Diane scrabbles and finds. Once she lopes twenty yards, having scented her prey under a boulder. The spring has perhaps gone a little from her step but then she has worked hard on a stomach increasingly bloated with croûtons and meat. All truffles found, the hunt ends. Diane gulps the remaining gobbets of meat. She has sniffed out perhaps eighty truffles and been deceived no more than half a dozen times. For staying out of her way, and for stamina in the cold, I am awarded a brace of muddy, knobby, odorous truffles.

They must be put in a basin and covered with soil, Monsieur Becquet instructs. Once gathered and exposed to the air, truffles begin to lose their flavour.

I bear the prize back to the flat. The only question, do we sell them and retire, or do we cook up a sauté of truffles Brillat-Savarin? We are in possession of something precious beyond rubies and deeply mysterious, like myrrh or mandragora or samples of the moon's surface. The family peers. I feel humble, like one of the Three Kings.

'C'est formidable!' murmurs Catherine in uncontrollable French.

'Yuk,' say the girls.

Children, what do they know?

Everyone in Catus seems to be on errands to Cahors. Next day outside the Tabac I am hailed by the Foissacs, the village schoolteachers. What news? they ask. We have two truffles, gathered yesterday, I say. We shall eat them, somehow, but without entering into anything too rarified, like truffled foie gras. Any suggestions?

'Eat them immediately!' cries Monsieur Foissac. Soil or no soil, the longer we keep them, the more they will lose their perfume, and beyond doubt we must do a truffled turkey. Alternatively, duck. He ponders on duck versus turkey. Ask a Frenchman a question about food and you are his prisoner until dusk.

Madame Foissac, while not pooh-poohing truffled duck or turkey, urges truffled omelettes, or baking the truffles in a wood fire. Wrap them in bacon and push them into the embers, she says. She begins to wax lyrical. 'Les truffes, ah, les plus nourissants des champignons!' The mud and grit must first be washed off. Colette, her favourite author, had washed truffles by dunking them in boiling champagne, but that, in Madame Foissac's view, had been extravagant, even ostentatious.

'Production is decreasing,' announces Monsieur Foissac with gloomy satisfaction. He quotes figures which cannot be confirmed, not here outside the Tabac, but he is confident of them. 'In Vaucluse half a century ago, seventy tons a year. Now, twenty. Did you know Louis XVIII ate a kilo of cooked truffles every evening? The farmers of the Lot don't eat a kilo in a lifetime. What they produce they sell. They produce fewer and fewer because they're too lazy to plant new truffle oaks.'

Madame Foissac, on the pavement, offers a recipe so elementary that there is no need for pencil and paper.

'Wash and slice the truffle, add it to beaten eggs, season with salt, and leave for three hours. Then cook as for scrambled eggs and – ça y est!'

That's what we'll do. Simplest is best. With our truffled eggs, salad, country bread, and Normandy butter, we drink, what else, a Vieux Cahors. All right, this red wine may be a little rich for so delicate an egg dish, and probably the wrong colour, but looked at from another angle, appropriate. The black wine of Cahors to wash down the black diamonds of Périgord, or in this case, the Lot. The scrambled eggs are a creamy, sloppy yellow – I like scrambled eggs sloppy – bejewelled with rubbery, black slivers of truffle, and hauntingly fragrant. Merci, Diane!

Lucy says, 'They taste like Mum's perfume smells.'

Nobody asked her. She's right, of course. She just didn't have to mention it. Arpège? One of the Chanels?

Kate wants to know why there are no potatoes. Polly is spreading her bread with butter and plum jam.

Stop Press: 1992.

1. Skulduggery in the truffle industry. *Le Monde* reports that truffle processing plants in Vaucluse are staining inferior white summer truffles with walnut juice bought from a chemicals company, disguising the bland taste with flavouring, and

selling them to fancy Paris restaurants as the pricier, black, Périgord truffles. The national fraud prevention office is sniffing and digging.

2. *The New York Times* reports from Cahors that technologists are working on an electronic nose which you carry on your shoulder and which will seek out truffles. At the town's Lycée Agricole a truffle expert believes that one day it may be possible to grow truffles like corn. In the meantime, a synthetic equivalent of the truffle fragrance has been developed and may soon be available in supermarkets, if it isn't already.

3. The price of one ounce of fresh Périgord truffles at Harrods is £28.00.

9 La Vie Bourgeoise

CATHERINE AND the girls have lit out to the Pyrenees
for the midterm break. Skiing. They are with a party
of fifty Cahors schoolchildren and a seasoning of teachers.
Gustave, a travelling man as well as a politician (looking after
coachloads of schoolchildren allows a teacher to see bits of
the world gratis) has gone along with sundry of his children.
How his bad back will hold up is his business. Catherine is
present as sous-chef, a ruse dreamed up by Gustave which will
allow an otherwise pricey holiday to pay for itself. She skis,
though, for the first time, the evidence being her limping
return to the rue Joffre, like Ashley returning to Tara in
Gone With the Wind. You don't acquire a limp like that
baking quiches and tossing fifty rounds of ground beef on
the grill.

Polly is limping too, and bandaged. Kate limps on both
ankles simultaneously and holds her hip. Nothing wrong with
Kate except an attack of the Sarah Bernhardts, though to be
on the safe side I fuss and sympathize. Both swear that skiing
is brilliant and they must go again, first opportunity. Lucy
is nonchalantly unmaimed, but she is expert, having skied
before, once.

Le patron, he too is fit, having stayed behind to work,
but so thrilled at being briefly solitary, answerable to no
one, that writer's block strikes and all he does is pace and
scratch himself. As confusing as this unfetteredness is the
March weather. Is it spring? The trees are bare, nights are

chilly, but on grassy roadside banks, in meadows and on the hills, are dandelions, daisies, primroses, and violets. I have taken walks and seen them. In the market appear the first daffs and anemones. London will now be a carpet of bugling daffodils, with tulips to come. Oh, to be in England, now that April's there, or soon will be. Not that I'm bereft. By positioning the radio on a particular radiator and twiddling the aerial I can just about hear the BBC. What I'd like is a short-wave set for the BBC World Service.

Away, defeatism, regret! Voluntarily to deracinate oneself from one's country, then grieve over what has been left behind – c'est idiot, ça! From such stirrings of misgiving is but a step to seeking out the British colony for bridge in the afternoons. Begone, base doubt!

Cotton dresses appear, the wolf whistlers with pots of paint on ladders shed their shirts, and for the first time in four months tables and chairs are hustled onto the pavements outside cafés. The next week is cold, wet, and wild. Then the sun bursts through again, and Lucy's friend, Marie-Claude, skips school one afternoon to sit in the park. People are taking to their beds with flu brought on, we are assured, by the bizarre weather. One morning our car refuses to start. 'Yours is not the only one, Monsieur,' the mechanic says darkly. He lifts the bonnet, performs a magician's flick with an oily rag, and voilà! the car starts.

Easter falls early in April. To escape the nonsense weather we drive on Good Friday the 250 miles to the Mediterranean for four or five days of guaranteed sun. It will make a change. I haven't seen outside the Lot for nine months. South through sleet and redbrick Albi, windshield wipers swishing. On to walled Carcassonne and, hey, sunshine! The landscape is uninterrupted vineyards, the mauve heights still further south are the Pyrenees. At Narbonne, then Perpignan, the wine-dark sea (in fact it's a shimmering blue) is flecked with a disturbing number of whitecaps.

We fetch up at dusk at Collioure, a fishing village on the Côte Vermeille, twelve miles from the Spanish border. A procession of penitents winds chanting through the alleys to the church. The penitents, in red-and-black robes, conical hats, and veils that mask their faces, carry flaming torches and lurid, bleeding effigies of the crucified Christ. At the windows are lighted candles, flowers, and the parchment faces of old women who rarely if ever bare their skin to the sun, unlike their fishermen husbands and sons, who seldom do anything else. The wind stabs like a Gascon's poniard.

Matisse, Picasso, Derain, and Dufy, were sometime inhabitants of Collioure, and before them the Greeks, Romans, Franks, and Spanish. No difficulty understanding why. Here are eucalyptus, palm, and orange trees, cliff scenery, and vistas of sea and mountain. Favorisé par un climat idéal, says the tourist brochure, and the summer flood of tourists may be imagined. The brochure fails to mention the tramontane, of which more in a moment.

Saturday morning. The sun is out, but the sea being of a temperature for polar bears, we take a walk along the coast road. Never have we walked more perilously. Not only does the wind pummel the ears and blind the eyes, but its violence is such that at each step we come close to being swept like litter over the cliffs and into the sea. This is the tramontane, a wind from the north as obnoxious as the mistral, maybe worse. The tramontane blows for two or three days, then ceases, we're told. Then it starts up again.

We see no profit hanging in here, making a study of the tramontane. Easy to see why the Greeks, Romans, Franks, Spanish, Matisse, Picasso, Derain and Dufy came to this coast, and easy to see why they left. By lunchtime Saturday we too have left, hurtling back to windless Cahors, and if need be in this neurotic springtime, our central heating.

The central heating is very much needed. On the morning of Easter Sunday, heading to the pâtisserie for the traditional coque de Pâques (Easter shell, though no one can explain why), we see that the hills are white. There is snow on the cars that have driven in from the countryside. In the market the talk is grim. This year's vines, peaches, plums, cherries, and early vegetables, or much of them, have been killed overnight by the cold. 'The coldest Easter in fifty years,' announces the radio.

We missed hot cross buns on Good Friday because we were on the road, so Catherine and the girls bake them now. They are spicier and tastier than the coque de Pâques, a pleasant enough but not hugely interesting brioche, glazed, sugared, studded with angelica, and no different from the Epiphany galettes, or, come to that, from the brioche loaves on sale daily in bakers' shops. At what further festivals, under what other names, will this sugary loaf present itself?

As if the spring weather were not perplexing enough, Lucy refuses to etch a cross on her hot cross buns, announcing that to do so would be hypocritical because she is not a believer. This we consider pompous but acceptable. The confusion arises when we find her with a girl friend on the Boulevard Gambetta handing out Christian tracts.

Confusion on confusion next weekend. We drive off for a couple of days to friends in Toulouse, without Lucy, who is invited to a vital birthday party (rabbit stew, stuffed cabbage, prune tart, no alcohol, and dancing). She will spend the night with her pal Marie-Claude and her parents, and has a key to our flat so she may return for the toothbrush, homework, and everything else she will forget. We instruct her that the party is not to move on to the flat and she is to admit no one in our absence.

On Sunday evening we return from Toulouse famished to find the cupboard bare. Bread, eggs, fruit, salad, cheese, everything that was to be our supper – all gone.

'Lucy, who's been here?'

'The Enfants de Dieu.'

'The who?'

'You know. They wander from town to town. They'd nowhere to sleep and they hadn't eaten for –'

'They *slept* here?'

'They made the beds and washed up all the dishes. They hadn't anywhere else to go. They stopped me on the boulevard . . .'

99

The Enfants de Dieu are a present-day equivalent of the mendicant friars of yore, except that they include girls as well as boys and often carry guitars. Not to mince matters, we're furious. How dared she admit total strangers who might have been, well, who knew what they might have been or perpetrated? To our surprise, Lucy hits back.

What right have we to deny supper and lodging to people who lead simple, good lives? We with our middle-class morality! We who put bourgeois crosses on our bourgeois hot cross buns! All we cared about was that the cheese was gone! The Enfants de Dieu live in the real world, the world of the spirit! Lucy storms to her room in tears.

She's right, of course, though the fact remains that the middle classes are supperless, and Kate and Polly complain that their beds smell odd. An hour or two pass before reconciliations take place.

Sprains and lumps from skiing plus a bout or two of flu reintroduce us to the French medical profession.

Two years ago we took Kate to the doctor in Catus. She was running a temperature and couldn't swallow. The doctor was a cheerful, handsome lad in a beat-up jersey who chain-smoked, lighting up each fresh Gauloise from the last, which he left in the brimming ashtray unextinguished, sending its fumey thread into the surgery, up Kate's nostrils, and down her throat. He diagnosed pharyngitis, scribbled down a dismaying list of medicaments, and as we were leaving, quoted his fee. In London, as I recall, on visits to the doctor, nothing so odious as actual money changes hands. ('Not sure I can change that. Hold on, here's a five. Do you have fifty p?') Here it does. C'est le commerce, as our Catus schoolteacher would say. And a pharmacy, we asked, where we could find these medicines? A côté, next door, Monsieur le Médecin said, utterly charming, exhaling Gauloise smoke. We didn't inquire if he were in cahoots with the pharmacist next door but we wondered. We bought the prescribed crateload of medicines from his accomplice, an alchemist in a white jacket, and two days later Kate was skipping, swimming, and eating everything set in front of her.

Each doctor we see in Cahors for these current ailments is thorough, friendly, and deeply respected in the community. All the ambitious adolescent offspring of people we know here aim to become doctors, or at second best dentists or veterinarians. No one has greater cachet in society than the doctor, or more money, other than rock stars and a few industrialists. After you have exposed your sprain or inflamed throat to this paragon, this nonpareil, and been rewarded with an exemplary diagnosis, the system rushes headlong into bureaucracy, but you quickly learn to bring along something to read.

You pay the doctor at the time of your visit. As the doctor shows no embarrassment, neither need the patient, though he might, I suppose, if he doesn't have the money. The doctor hands over a signed form with prescriptions for medicines, of which there are a great number. You seek out a pharmacy, readily discoverable because outside every pharmacy is its green and white emblem, a snake coiled round a cross, and more than likely a pharmacy will be adjacent to the doctor's office. The majority of items on the list – I am sorry to say this but see no way round it – are suppositories to insert up your backside. The French believe that by this route the medicine infuses the system quicker and more efficaciously. We Brits take our medicine orally, the French anally. No future in being ill and squeamish in France.

For the French, suppositories; for the British and Dutch, pills; for the Germans, injections. The medicine prescribed depends on the national obsession with whatever organ and the ailment that derives from it. The Germans consume great quantities of heart medication because they are particularly fearful of the heart and circulation. They, the Swiss, and central Europeans, go first for herbal remedies and hot and cold baths. They accept antibiotics only if herbs and baths fail. In Britain and the United States we consume antibiotics because the cause of illness is an external agent, the bacterium, and because, in Britain especially, we are obsessed with the stomach. In France and southern Europe the seat of well-being, or of the malady, is the liver. Whatever the ailment in France, its origin is the liver, la foie, as in crise de foie, literally a liver crisis (not to be muddled with the ejaculation, Ma foi! – My faith!). Frequently we hear of Cadurciens laid low by a crise de foie. Our compatriots are much tickled because a crise de foie – biliousness, nausea – derives from excess, usually over-indulgence in food and drink. Of the competing opinions, liver versus stomach, the latter is the likelier as a source of fatigue, so medical intelligence has it, or this week it does. The liver is the reason you are fatigued in France. In Britain it is probably because you are depressed, in which case you should pull your socks up. In Germany it is cardiac insufficiency. In America it's a virus.

If this run-down on cultural differences in health smacks of egregious generalizing, how dull life would be without the generalization.

So, having made sure the pharmacist has legibly written (some hope) on the form the name and price of each medicine, and signed it, you gather up the medicines and pay the pharmacist his or her fortune. At home you peel away the little sticky ticket on each box, bottle, vial and tub of suppositories, unguents, etc., and transfer it to the doctor's form. The tickets adhere reasonably efficiently, like postage stamps. You do this because if you don't you won't be reimbursed. You also enter on the form a certain amount of your personal history, and sign it.

This form, smothered in tickets, signatures, and comical squiggles from the doctor, you bear off to the social security office together with the relevant Common Market identity forms (you know about those, surely?) showing that you qualify for reimbursement. Inside the social security office you pick up a numbered ticket like a betting slip from an official in a glass cage. Then you find a seat and open your book. If the book is Berlitz's *French for Travellers* you can revise the Doctor section, e.g. Quelque chose m'a piqué (I've been stung).

When your number is called you present your documents at a counter, retire, and carry on revising. At the calling of your name you proceed to the cash desk, sign your name, and scoop up your reimbursement. This will be some seventy-five per cent of what you paid the doctor and pharmacist (much less for dentists' and opticians' fees). You now jaunt humming and jingling out of the social security office and into the nearest bar.

French doctors have our seal of approval. Yet, as anywhere, there are those whom you'd be happy to bop on the nose. Kate is no Amazon. She weighs probably much the same as a netful of the butterflies that are beginning to reappear along the river bank. Today, she tells us, the school doctor on his routine visit said, 'You should take some exercise. Next.' The impudence! Kate swims, skis, somersaults round the gym, and now goes horseback riding once a week. All three girls would ride every day were it possible. They cavort at pop concerts and dance at discos.

Lucy returns from a pop concert with a poster of a bespangled singer which she pins to the wall of her room.

'Good singer?' we inquire.

'Great,' she says.

'French – all in French?'

'Of course. Except now and then he shouted "Right!" and "Boogie-woogie!".'

Boogie-woogie? We thought boogie-woogie had gone out around 1948. Either France's pop scene is behind the times or it knows something we don't.

On May Day the market does a brisk business in lilies of the valley. The tradition is to give a sprig of lily of the valley to a loved one: husband or wife, boyfriend or girlfriend. We return from springtime walks in the hills with wild flowers for the sitting room and the kitchen table. This amuses the French, who decorate their homes with cultivated flowers exclusively.

Outside every house is a square or circular flower bed. Those in the countryside have protective wire netting to keep the ducks and chickens out. Wild flowers are of no interest to the French unless they can be eaten or drunk.

Men's Fashion Note: Handbags are in. Styling varies little – flattish, black leather receptacles about ten inches by six inches with a zip or buckle and a thong for the wrist. I might invest in one. They are sensible and not considered effeminate. Not every man carries a handbag, they are not obligatory, but they are everywhere to be seen in hairy hands. We have spotted one carried by a uniformed gendarme. An acquaintance who knows Italy tells us that handbags for men are even more common there. She says this is because Italian men wear such tight pants that they are unable to put anything in the pockets.

Voting day in municipal elections throughout France, always a Sunday, is no concern of ours except as observers. As our kitchen window looks down on the courtyard of the town hall, we watch the townspeople queuing outside the salle de vote. Umbrellas lift against the rain. In the hiatus between mass and Sunday lunch the queue swells. All is orderly, not a policeman in sight. Everyone knows someone in the queue, and there's much handshaking, hat-raising, and chatter. Gustave is not re-elected and says he's not surprised. The election fizzed with scheming and in-fighting.

The following Saturday we visit Catus. There the establishment has been re-elected in its entirety. But for the first time in many years three or four opposition candidates stood and today they are celebrating with an alfresco feast for friends and supporters. In the Lot even a defeat is a cause for celebration. They have dug a trench and are roasting a whole lamb over a wood fire. Whole roast lamb is the celebration par excellence. Apart from truffles, and maybe preserved duck, only two delicacies compete: couscous and onion soup. The Lot gastronomes are convinced that onion soup is unique to the region.

At midnight we find ourselves in the booming trembling village hall of another village, celebrating the re-election of the mayor, a bright-eyed, tortoise-skinned winegrower who has been mayor for forty years – half his life. We are too late for the banquet, mercifully, but mousseux is poured for us. All three hundred inhabitants of the village are present, rock music pounds through loudspeakers, the floor quakes, and everyone dances except babes in arms, octogenarians (such as the mayor), and those flushed farmers who have fallen asleep. Catherine asks the mayor to dance. Consternation! He protests that he has not danced for a quarter of a century. Finally, twinkling, waving like royalty to the applause, he accepts. He is a head and a half shorter than Catherine, but mobile, and after the dance, back at the becrumbed, wine-ringed trestle table, he holds her hand, introduces her in patois to mobs of friends, and twinkles and sparkles like the mousseux.

A handkerchief is passed among the assembly. Whoever has the handkerchief when the music stops must choose someone to kiss. The pair kneel, the handkerchief on the floor between them, and kiss. Cheering and whistling! The music starts up, the handkerchief circulates, the game continues. At three o'clock we thank the mayor, congratulate him again on his election victory, and totter into the night. The festivities will go on until dawn, and the mayor will be last to leave.

10 Landscape with Figures

W E ARE to star in a French film. I am pretty blasé about it, being aware of the fleetingness of fame, and having read how stars must arrive on the set at five in the morning then twiddle their thumbs all day while the director sorts out camera angles and waits for the wind to drop.

Star isn't quite the word. We are to be a segment in a publicity film the French Tourist Board is making for its rural holiday homes known as gîtes. In their wisdom the film makers from Paris want a shot of an English family driving up in an English car to a gîte which is a converted windmill near Cajarc, thirty kilometres east, where Françoise Sagan was born and President Pompidou had a holiday home. Someone – we suspect Elizabeth, head of our France-Great Britain Association and casting director manqué – has passed them our name. No fee will come our way. On the other hand we don't have to show up until ten.

Our car happens to be French. As it comes with a right-hand drive for the British market, and British registration, the director thinks it will do. He wears designer denim and sunglasses. Our impression is of a film crew on a tight schedule with a good many more gîtes to be filmed.

Though high summer, the day is so gloomy and cold that after studying the slate sky through his sunglasses the director decides to start with interiors. This evidently means an English family enjoying a typical meal in their holiday windmill. We wait two hours while sound and lighting equipment are positioned in the windmill's kitchen, but we grow colder and colder. When our moment of immortality arrives we are asked to remove our jerseys and jackets so that audiences won't mistake the windmill for an igloo, and to act out an English family enjoying a typical holiday meal. Wine, cake, and a salami have been set on the table. The director invites me to smile and pour the Vin de Cahors, showing the label, then sip it. 'Quiet please, take one, roll 'em!' he calls out in French, or words to that effect. Stage fright and the arctic cold have by now taken such a grip that my hand shakes like a leaf in the wind. Vin de Cahors slops on the table when I pour and down my shirt when I sip. Any audience viewing this tourist film will assume that the English holidaymaker is on his second bottle at least. Catherine, chilled to the bone, wearing a fixed smile, carves the cake. Given the day off school, the girls sit and shiver. I await the director's cry, 'Cut!', and orders to rehearse, then do it all again, but evidently that's it. Is he happy? Is he intending to use this mealtime sequence in the Lot windmill? The sun never does come out, and the shot of an English family driving up with their right-hand drive isn't attempted. Whether French tourism bureaux round the world are to this day screening an English family with wooden grins in a windmill, red wine splashing through the air, I have no idea.

Adieu, stardom.

More excitement. We are invited to a wedding. Remember right-wing Raymond and Ginette, forgers of identity cards, in their château with the mouroir to which they will repair to die? Raymond's son, born on the wrong side of the blanket in Raymond's rakehell youth, pre-Ginette, is to wed a lass from Bordeaux.

The ceremony takes place in the village church, overlooked by the turreted château, at five on a sunny Saturday afternoon. The radiant bride holds a single pink rose. The groom, in a sombre suit, is scrubbed, nervous, and looks about fourteen (he is twenty-six). A pathway of strewn

107

boxwood leaves leads to the church doors, which remain open throughout the ceremony, letting in butterflies, wasps, and summery smells. Tipsy, the mongrel from the château, is well behaved, investigating side chapels and sniffing each of the fifty guests prior to the service, but thereafter sitting at the feet of his master, the groom's father (former libertine). A greater distraction than Tipsy is a half-sister of the groom. She tiptoes round the happy couple, past the altar, behind the priest, and back on the same circuit, and alternative circuits, taking flash photographs. In lieu of choir and organ we have tentative hymns *a capella*. A collection plate circulates. In his homily the priest compares marriage with wine and its harvest: the need for daily care and nurturing, the guarding against squally weather, the slow maturing, and the joy of a fine vintage achieved after love and affection.

The hours between the ceremony and supper at eight-thirty are slow-maturing indeed, there being nothing to eat or drink, no speeches or reading of telegrams or inspecting of presents, and not a thing to do except stand on the lawn of the eighteenth century château looking at the flowers and offering best wishes to the bride and groom. This blank period ends with a move to the château's cellars where at four that morning the groom's father had cemented the final paving stone. Spread out over tables is a cold buffet from a caterer: pâtés and hams, beef and chicken, mountains of tomatoes, salad and cheese. The pièce montée is pyramids of choux pastry balls filled with crème pâtissière, each pyramid surmounted by a figurine of a wedding couple. The wine flows from barrels of local red. We also have soft drinks, sangría, one or two bottles of spirits, and an unexpected cask of Bordeaux.

The bride's mother, a Bordelaise, has contributed the Bordeaux so that we of the Lot may enjoy a real wine. 'You drink the Bordeaux?' inquires the bride's mother, touring and raising her voice above the din of music and dancing that has started through the arched stone entrance into an adjacent cellar. 'You must drink the Bordeaux – it is better!' She is a formidable, if repetitive, champion of the wine of her region.

Apart from the singing, dancing, eating, and kissing of the bride, there are animated conversations and monologues. A flushed young man harangues me on the merits of Gide. I overhear Catherine and the groom's father in debate on the Romanesque architecture of certain Lot churches. One disc follows another onto the record player. The dancers hop and whirl. 'You are drinking the Bordeaux?' asks the bride's mother, plucking my sleeve and peering into my paper cup. Her own cup holds a bubbly, brownish liquid.

'Mais qu'est-ce que c'est que ça, Madame?'

'Whiskey et Coca-Cola,' the bride's mother says with a startled, guilty look.

Less thrilling than a wedding or being filmed in a windmill is the July day when I rise and go down to the street to collect our emptied garbage pail. It has not been emptied. Is today Sunday?

Electricity, gas, water, telephone, ambulance, police – all services in Cahors run with becoming smoothness, and none more so than refuse collection, six days a week. Should you happen to stay a night or two in Cahors, find a back room away from the street, otherwise, except on Sunday, you will be awakened at five-thirty by the crashing of trash cans and whistling of dustmen.

Today is not Sunday. Today is Le Quatorze Juillet. July 14. No dustmen and no anybody. The shops are shut, the streets empty. Bastille Day, la fête nationale, and Cahors is dead.

At ten o'clock the town is still dead. I find an open baker's, but where are the parades, fireworks, champagne, dancing in the streets? An area in front of Gambetta's statue is cordoned off and the Tricolour flaps in anticipation, but in anticipation of what and when? I try the Hôtel de Police and am told the ceremony took place at nine-thirty. A brief ceremony, apparently: the mayor and one or two functionaries, a squad of soldiers, the town band playing the *Marseillaise*. At least I have been spared the town band.

What next then on this Quatorze Juillet? At what hour, Monsieur, the fireworks and revelry?

No fireworks this year, not in Cahors, the policeman believes. A ball though, at ten tonight in the Place Général de Gaulle.

Good, good – and between now and ten tonight?

The policeman shrugs his Gallic shrug and looks through the window at the ashen sky. He supposes most people will be indoors watching television.

Television, not that we have one, is the surest way of capturing the essence of this national holiday, at least in Cahors. All morning one of the channels relays a military parade from Paris, and the President receiving guests at the Elysée Palace. We catch a bite of it chez Elizabeth and Jean. In Cahors there is nothing from the time of the swift ceremony at the Gambetta statue in the morning until the dancing that night in the Place Général de Gaulle. In several outlying villages are fireworks and public roastings of lamb. At least the rain holds off for the ten o'clock ball. Two to three hundred men, women, children, and dogs, leave television to talk and dance in front of a stage from which shrills an amplified accordion band.

By the by, should you happen to be in Paris on the night of Bastille Day, avoid the Place de la Bastille, the most obvious place to be. I have been there so I know. The place is crowded and they throw fireworks at you. They throw them at your feet, through café doors, and under the table where you sit. Who is 'they'? How do I know who? French juveniles with too many fireworks.

For three weeks before, on, and after Bastille Day, the media occupy themselves with France's greatest and noisiest single sporting event, a bicycle race. The Tour de France consists of a hundred men in gaudy jerseys pedalling like the wind round France, and often taking in corners of Spain, Italy, Switzerland, Luxembourg, Belgium, and Holland. Accompanying them is a bleating cavalcade of team managers, doctors and journalists in cars, and stereophonic vans selling magazine subscriptions and insurance, and tossing leaflets and samples of coffee beans to the populace lining the road. Woe betide you if you happen to be motoring on the same road! Police will divert you left, right, or back whence you came. 'C'est le commerce,' predictably observes our schoolmaster friend from Catus. Indeed it is, but the Tour de France is also a sport which each July puts millions of French in a fever.

Millions of others, I suspect, remain indifferent. Not one of our friends knows or cares who is winning, or if they do they are not admitting it. Of course, if one year the Tour is routed through Cahors, and whirls along the Boulevard Gambetta, there'll be no ignoring it then.

The school year is over. Swimsuits and beach balls beckon from the shelves at Prisunic. Also the folding picnic tables and chairs essential to French families on the road. Just off the road, within inches of streaming traffic, families set up the furniture and open the hamper. Why they never take a side road and picnic in an unpolluted meadow is an enigma. I can only guess that they enjoy a sense of vacation togetherness from their closeness to fellow travellers on the road.

Lucy has passed her exams but is disgruntled. How, she wants to know, could she have scored only eighty-five per cent in her oral English? The English of the examiner, a Frenchwoman, had been good, she tells us, but anyone could tell she wasn't English. She had said zis, zat, zose. I can't become excited over the unjust eighty-five per cent. These exams are not vital, unlike the baccalauréat to come, so we hardly want to make an issue of it, take it up with the school board. I settle for the shrug and splayed palms, held for a count of five, and 'C'est la vie'. This seems to satisfy Lucy.

Kate and Polly have had tests in French, maths, history, and geography. As they have tests almost daily they remain immune to debilitating anxiety, or seem to. Some of their marks fail to scintillate. Two out of twenty in French? But that's absurd, they are fluent! Their teachers should hear them sing the bouncy French winner of the Eurovision Song Contest! *Comme un enfant ta TA ta ta TA ta.* They sing it from start to finish, except it never finishes. Either it has seventy verses or it is circular, restarting the instant it ought to expire. *Comme un oiseau ta TA ta ta TA ta.* They sing it through the flat, down the stairs, and along the rue Joffre. What please is the French for earplugs and where might we buy them?

Taufik has dropped from sight. New names are bruited. Michel, Antoine, Robert, Jean-Louis. O female fickleness! In fact, those names are discussed less frequently than Zazie, Duke, Hector, and Bijou. These are horses. As often as their *sous* allow, Kate and Polly are off to the stables. So who did you ride today? 'Bijou – he was hopeless, zut, everybody *hates* Bijou!' Without *sous* they go anyway to muck out, to groom Bijou, and they return noisomely scented. They have become Thelwell cartoon girls in jodhpurs and second-hand riding caps, incipient Princess Annes, worshippers of the bridle and bit, passionate for the reek of tackle and hay, and gleefully terrorised by the gallop and the ditch to be jumped.

Without the girls, who have better things to do, Catherine and I tramp the chalky hills by ourselves or with friends: Elizabeth, Gustave, Ginette and Raymond, Françoise and Gimi. This is walking country, guided if you wish by the booklet of randonnées, walks, some of two kilometres, others of twenty and fifty, the route signalled by red arrows painted on trees and walls. The fields and hedges blaze with oxeye daisies, poppies, eglantine, honeysuckle, mallow, wild garlic, hollyhocks, foxgloves, and orchids. Botanists from faraway countries come to the Lot for the orchids. One orchid looks exactly like a bumble bee. Underfoot are wild strawberries. The air smells of mint, thyme, and lavender, and is loud with twittering birdsong and the sawing of cicadas. To either side of butterfly-filled tracks and pathways are unkempt fields divided by low limestone walls – until suddenly appears a kempt field yellow with sunflowers, or grazed by sheep. On a wall at a crossroads stands an iron crucifix. Rusting among nettles lie ploughs and harrows forsaken by families who have given up and left, hoping for greener grass on the other side of the hill. In fields too small or steep for tractors are unrusted ploughs towed by oxen or horses. In the cultivated oblongs of fields bordering the rivers, farmers in their working blues and berets, and their wives in straw hats, drive the oxen, hoe the soil, and scatter seed from paper bags. They are figures in a landscape by Corot.

Are they also the French farmers who protest against low subsidies and cheap imports by blocking roads with their pigs and tractors, and by vandalizing lorry loads of fruit from Spain, and tankers from Italy, emptying thousands of gallons of decent Italian wine into the ground? Impossible.

We haven't a lot of time to find out. Out of the blue has come an invitation to teach in the United States, on Long Island, starting in September. We brew tea, bring out the atlas, and convene a family council. What about the friends we shall be leaving behind, not to mention the bread?

But it's only for a year. We can return to the Lot. The glamour of the New World wins. Five to none in favour.

A disappointment has been that in Cahors, for the first time, the girls have not much enjoyed school. Kate and Polly don't have a wealth of experience of school, but Lucy is expert enough. To date she has attended seven schools in five countries. Here at the Collège Gambetta she has relentless homework, the translating of Caesar's battle plans at weekends, and hour-long classes which seem, she says, to go on for ever.

In London classes lasted forty minutes. Not that she complains. But the opinion of the girls is that school in Cahors lacks lightness, it's predictable and tough, and they'd not say no to a change.

One reason for fleeing London was the hurly-burly – some might term it rat race – for winning entry into the more desirable middle-class schools: the applications and interviews, the conducted tours in the company of competing parents, the vetting and being vetted, wearing one's most careful Professor Higgins accent, and presenting one's offspring as paragons who could not but further burnish the school's reputation for excellence, a challenge best met by keeping them out of sight. By escaping that, we have found ourselves in a rigidly structured academic system which emphasizes grammar and mathematics. Goody. Reading, writing, and 'rithmetic, the basics. But of the creative stuff, barely a glimmer. No music – the Fulham school shook with choirs and bands – and exiguous art, debate, anything at all titillating the imagination. The French system seems designed for the manufacture of scholars. If this is the case, it doesn't succeed, as far as we can tell. Much of the classwork and homework involves memorizing French irregular verbs, mathematical formulae, and paragraphs from history and geography textbooks. Too many staff seem bent on discouraging rather than encouraging their charges. A child with consistently poor marks redoubles, which is to say stays down in the class for a further year. A pupil aged seventeen or eighteen who has redoubled and redoubled might find himself in a class of fifteen-year-olds.

From the start stress is placed on impeccable, symmetrical handwriting. No bad thing as long as leeway is allowed for a quirky letter y here; an individualistic capital G there, but it isn't. Victor Hugo, France's greatest poet, said, 'Symmetry is tedious, and tedium is the very basis of mourning. Despair yawns.' He may not have had in mind handwriting as taught in the Lot but he could have.

The sunnier side is that Kate has been made to learn a poem by Victor Hugo which, years on, she still enjoys and is able to spout, melancholy affair though it is: twelve lines of the poet walking to Harfleur to put holly and heather on the grave of his daughter, Léopoldine, drowned in the Seine. In history she has learned something of the twentieth century and is aware that in her grandfathers' lifetime two world wars have been fought. This pleases me. For three years from the age of nine, at school in Yorkshire, and with a new teacher each year, all I learned of history was Stone Age Man. Could it have been that Stone Age Man was all the teachers knew? I became a virtuoso in the drawing of flint-head axes.

We pack. A man with a satchel and clipboard arrives to read the metres. We ask the estate agent to retrieve for us, please, the deposit we put down on the flat. Is that a tic beneath his eye or did he flinch? He says he'll do his best. Friends tell us we will never see the deposit. French landlords – ours is a landlady but they are the same, if not worse, we're told – never return the deposit. We don't believe it. We are leaving the flat in better shape than we found it.

Those friends with time, muscle, and spare rope, are corralled into assisting in lowering the tables and beds from the windows in the rue Joffre, to be returned to the Samaritans who lent them. We have too many invitations to goodbye dinners of excessive food and wine. We'll be back, we assure Elizabeth and Jean, Raymond and Ginette, Françoise and Gimi, Jeff and Sally, Gustave, Sylvette, the Wolfes, the Foissacs, Madame Radiguet, et al, though we haven't the least idea whether we will or not.

11 Bed and Breakfast

ENOUGH FOR the moment of us Brits in the Lot. While the family pack train is off and away to Long Island, birthplace of Walt Whitman ('I sound my barbaric yawp over the roofs of the world'), what about the French abroad?

How does Jean-François in Britain take to our food and language? And Hans and Giuseppe, come to that. Do they suffer the meals in silence? Send back the meat and two veg and the jam roll as inedible? Clap their hands and call for the recipe?

Catherine and I are experts. For two years before emigrating to the Lot we received into our home in gentrified Bowerdean Street, Fulham, not a few Frenchmen (one at a time), also Germans, Italians, and Spaniards. They were junior executives sent by their companies to a two-week crash-course in English at a high-octane language school off Kensington High Street. More or less willingly they dropped from the sky, strangers in a strange land, and for two gruelling weeks fought with irregular verbs and the pronunciation of 'this', 'that' and 'those'. The cowardly stayed at hotels. Others, ambitious to practise their English at all times, and paying a fifth of what a hotel would have cost, opted for one of the listed families offering bed, breakfast, and 'occasional evening meals at £2'. Two pounds were two pounds in the early seventies, and ours was not the only home competing for this extra pocket money. Bowerdean Street alone had three such families. Some of the business types the school sent to us were highly entertaining. Others were a pain in the neck.

Claude, an otherwise bashful computer programmer from Paris, ate unbashfully with the appetite of a Bermondsey docker and wiped his plate to a high polish with bread. Klaus, from Stuttgart, announced on his second day, 'The English terrible cooks are.' He would turn up his nose at roast pork, lamb kebabs, harmless tuna salad with artichoke hearts, and pile his plate with potatoes.

Claude was our first junior executive and so shy that we would forget he was in the house. He would steal in invisibly every evening after school, then appear at eight for dinner, smiling, blinking, leaning forward slightly from the waist, and we would smile and blink back, wondering who he was. He was dapper with shiny pink cheeks and looked about sixteen. In fact he had four children, the eldest fifteen. On the table by his bed he had positioned framed photographs of his family.

We knew about the photographs because Catherine entered the room to vacuum and dust. Everything in Claude's room was meticulous – English dictionaries, notebooks and pens lined up like data in a computer – except the bed, which had not been made and never was. Experience taught us that Continental men may be divided into bedmakers and non-bedmakers, the latter being the larger group.

Claude arrived with gifts of perfume and duty-free whisky and for two weeks he was appreciative and undemanding. He took his evening meal with us regularly. Between courses he would respond in slow, inaccurate English to questions about computers, Paris, his family, and his day at the school. When the soup, fish or salad arrived, conversation came to a halt because he would lower his head and fall upon the food with such gusto that not only was his mouth too full for speaking but he no longer heard anything said to him. He liked it all: steaks, liver, sardines, beetroot, lentils, moussaka, haddock soufflé, Irish soda bread, and shop-bought sliced bread like coir matting. He would drink two glasses of wine, never more, never less, and dab his mouth vigorously with his napkin after each swallow. He did not eat butter or a cooked

117

breakfast. We had expected a headlong plunge into bacon and eggs but he wanted only bread, jam, and tea. He was apprehensive of Kate and Polly, then aged nine and seven, who soon gave up following him and trying to amuse him with jokes.

Only in his leaving us was Claude less than a success. He had a seat on the first morning flight out of Heathrow to Paris so needed a taxi at the house at 5.45 a.m. We warned Claude that any taxi we ordered the night before might or might not show up and if it didn't he must wake me up and I would lead him fast to the likeliest corner for a roving taxi. At 5.46 a.m. Claude awoke us with quiet but persistent knocking. There he was, pink and dressed for travel, leaning forward from the waist, and in a suppressed state of panic. Three minutes later, with still no sign of the taxi (it never did arrive), I set off with Claude at a gallop for the New King's Road, carrying, as a hostly gesture, his suitcase, which he had packed with souvenirs made entirely of lead. We found a taxi, thanks be to God. Glistening with sweat, waving through the window, Claude was swept away. Not until a week later did the girls realize that he had gone.

Alain, a scientist at Aérospatiale in Toulouse – the first Concorde, built by his company and BAC, made its maiden fight from Toulouse – was another family man who never made his bed. Sod them all, let him make his own bed, I would command Catherine. Their bed being made for them was just what these executive juveniles didn't need if they were to grow up. Catherine made the bed, for whatever reason; perhaps motherliness in part, and disliking the thought of an unmade bed in the house, but mainly for fear of the client complaining to the school, which could mean no more clients and no more pocket money. Alain took substantial first and second helpings and, like Claude, polished his plate to a spotless gloss. 'Is very nice, I like,' he would say, quaffing liberally of red wine at twice the price the same plonk would cost in Toulouse. He would empty the casserole of the beef and kidney stew we had hoped might stretch to the girls' supper next day. Alain was a big rumpled man with a black

118

beard and a black polo-neck jersey which he wore every day for two weeks. He was full of appetite and bounce, or as full as exhausting days at the language school allowed him to be. At Aérospatiale he probably burst with vitality but a foreign language is a great, debilitating leveller.

All our guests were to a greater or lesser extent crushed by the effort demanded by the crash-course. They set out fairly breezily after breakfast in the expectation that today could not possibly be as bad as yesterday, and in the evening slunk back whipped and beaten. After an hour to themselves and an apéritif, and encouraged by chat with their host couple, who were concentrating too hard on understanding the guest's English to bother correcting grammar and vocabulary, the colour would come back to their cheeks, and in Alain's case some of his bounce would return. During and between courses Alain would talk about Toulouse, his favourite dish (cassoulet), whether he should join the school's optional outing to Cambridge, and what appropriately British presents we thought he should take back to his family. When stuck for the right word his bounce would be transmuted into despair and he would gasp and beat his forehead with his fists.

Unlike many of our customers he tried to converse with the girls. He grimaced and smote his temples from the strain of it while Catherine tried to assure him that children were impossibly difficult to understand in a foreign language, especially Polly, who spoke faster than anyone in the world. Everyone worked very hard. Polly worked tirelessly, gazing into Alain's eyes and repeating over and over, 'Wha's-yellow-'n'-goes-round'-'n'-roun'?' The colour would mount in her cheeks as her frustration grew. Alain would tug at his beard and bang his skull as the small girl, now shouting – 'Wha's-yellow-'n'-goes-roun'-'n'-roun'!'– endeavoured to penetrate his deafness. Close to tears, red frustrated face close to his, suddenly she would shout out, 'Banana-in-a-washing-machine!', believing that if he could not understand the question, he might at least understand the answer.

Alain had an irritating habit of bouncing into the kitchen while I was cooking and hanging over my shoulder. Normally

Catherine cheffed but I coped with breakfast, usually a hit-and-run affair of tea, toast and cereal, but for Alain, at his request, the full English fry-up. (Still, simpler than the alternative of organizing the children, cat, guinea-pigs, goldfish, milkman, etc.) Our kitchen was an extension of the dining-room, and if Alain's breakfast was not on the table when he made his entrance, as it never was, he would bounce to the stove, shake hands, and thrust his bearded face into the frying pan, uttering grunts of approval and anticipation. He scrutinized each elementary operation performed with oil, eggs, bacon, salt, pepper, parsley, and coffee-grinder, totally failing to interpret the silence that was the breakfast cook's response. Apart from a reluctance to be seen bringing out yesterday's leftover potatoes for frying up, I had no good reason to be irritated by Alain's presence at the stove. Master chefs at the Tour d'Argent are presumably unmoved by trainees clustering round. But the closer to the frying-pan Alain dipped his beard, the crosser I became.

No leftover potatoes when Klaus was our customer. Klaus was a German potato-fiend who ate every potato in sight. He arrived not for the mere two-week language course but for a rare four-week course. Moreover, he walked in with his baggage on the same day as another four-week student, a Spanish banker named Francisco. The school had telephoned to say August was an emergency, could we take two students? My golly, we would be rich! We gave our own room to Klaus and despatched ourselves to the basement. Whatever else, Klaus and Francisco would make a change from the French.

Klaus was in the legal department of a West German automobile company. He told a long story about how he had flown one Christmas to Barcelona to examine an alleged defect in a Mercedes, then couldn't get home because of snow on the runway. We were surprised he hadn't skied home as he was extremely athletic. He might have been still more athletic but for weak eyesight (he wore thick, intimidating glasses) and a bad back (like Gustave), the result of a car smash in his younger days as a racing motorist. He had also lost the third finger of his left hand. The empty space between the second and fourth fingers fascinated Polly. She would turn up during the evening meal, when she should have been in bed, and stare wonderingly at the space.

Klaus studied prepositions and tenses during breakfast (cooked) and in the evening would plant himself at the dining-room table, clear a space, and write out lists of vocabulary. Unless it was to borrow a glass for the packs of lager he brought back and carried up to his room, he never crossed the border into the kitchen. He was by no means humourless, so we were faintly stunned when on the second evening he declared, 'The English terrible cooks are,' and did not appear to be making a joke. We were eating a perfectly presentable kidneys à la Bordelaise. The previous evening we had had grilled mackerel with gooseberry sauce and he had left almost all of that too, for which the cat at least was grateful. Groping for clues as to what he might enjoy, we dropped such words as Sauerkraut and Schnitzel but Klaus's eyes failed to light up. We telephoned a friend, Shirley, one of only four teachers of German shorthand in London, and asked her what Germans ate. 'Potatoes,' Shirley said. We said, 'What besides potatoes?' 'Nothing besides,' she said. 'Just potatoes.' So when Klaus dined in, which was most evenings for four weeks, we gave him potatoes. Potatoes boiled, baked, creamed, roasted, sautéed, french fried, and we'd have offered the Carême recipe where you pound them with butter, eggs, sugar, and flour, and shape then into little boats, except that Klaus seemed already bewildered enough by the unrelenting cavalcade of potatoes. We would discover that the only potatoes he had met before were boiled potatoes. 'Baked pot-a-to, pot-a-to in ja-cket,' he would echo, marvelling, peeling away and discarding the skin. We have yet to meet a Continental European who will eat the skin, the best part.

And where was our banker, Francisco, all this time? Usually out shopping. Francisco was pale, black-haired, and out of condition. Except for puddings, the more synthetic the better, he was not much interested in food, but he drank copiously of water, always a full tumbler before eating, again when he had finished, and whenever he passed near a tap.

His rushing, rustling, half-swallowed phrases and incomplete sentences sounded to our ears like Spanish, though Klaus, who came to know him better than we did, assured us they were English. We had not known there are no sibilants in Spanish – none in Francisco's Spanish anyway – but there is considerable lisping. As he had introduced himself as Franthithco, Kate and Polly assumed that was his name and called him Franthithco. To avoid confusion, for four weeks we all addressed him as Franthithco.

Franthithco haunted the shops of the West End for bargains, particularly in electronic equipment. His chief disappointment was that they were not open all night as evidently they are in Spain. The locking of doors at six o'clock limited much of his shopping to window-shopping, and when late at night the lights in the windows went out, then some of the street lights, he would limp back to us and drink three or four tumblers of water. Other language students straggled back wearied by learning. Franthithco returned wearied by shopping.

His first acquisition was a collapsible umbrella which folded into itself and sprang open like a flick-knife at the touch of a button. At that epoch such umbrellas were a novelty which had not yet reached Spain. Franthithco was delighted with it. He said he had bought it from a man on the pavement in Oxford Street.

He was more doubtful about the tartan skirt he bought for his wife. He had talked for days about what to buy her, studying his notes and totting up sums on his calculator. He liked the idea of tartan but was uncertain about the size, and he would hold up the skirt in the dining-room, seeking reassurance in his rustling English. With the umbrella and the tartan skirt he might have been planning a family trip to Scotland.

His big buys were in electronics, chiefly hi-fi equipment, stereos and loudspeakers from the cut-price stores on Tottenham Court Road. These were cheaper than in Spain, he told us. There was also the matter of duty and customs which he would evade by shipping the equipment to a contact in Bilbao, then transporting it overland. When he had visited the Canary Islands the best buy had been colour television sets, he told us, and he had shipped two to a contact in Cadiz, then by car to his home. Franthithco paid no income tax and was astonished to learn that we did. No one in Spain paid income tax, he said. Yes, there were income-tax *laws*, but there were ways of skirting them, especially if you were a banker.

Vans started to arrive at the house and unload containers filled with electronic equipment. We admitted the containers to the house but thereafter preferred to know as little as possible. We would hear Franthithco thumping about among the containers in his room upstairs, binding them with ropes, and forging customs declarations. I had visions of undercover carabineros from Madrid driving up to the house and carrying him off in manacles to undergo the bastinado.

Apart from cans of lager and knick-knacks for his wife and daughter, Klaus made only two significant purchases. One was a trendy denim suit, the other a pair of streamlined, Wimbledon-type tennis rackets. 'Cheaper than in Germany,' he said, and more or less commanded me to play tennis with him. He gave me a thrashing, unbothered by poor eyesight, spinal injury, and missing finger.

At the end of four weeks Klaus and Franthithco presented us with flowers and a flagon of wine. Seeing them into a taxi we suffered a small pang, though neither had been a bedmaker.

Otto, a research chemist from Zürich, arrived bearing gifts of flowers, liquor, perfume, and lavish beribboned Swiss chocolates for the girls. His English was good, he was well informed on all subjects, he enjoyed his meals, complimented the chef, worked hard, drank little, smoked not at all, was organized, friendly, willing, clean, reliable, and made his bed. Three days it took us to put a finger on the snag. He was a master bore.

Otto never gave me or anyone a chance to show how boring we could be because he talked into and through all opposition, very leadenly, getting his subordinate clauses correct, saying 'whom', unstoppable as a battle tank.

I don't know what he talked about. Everything, anything. Usually himself. He was desperately fluent. Our food would cool on our plates while we waited for him to shut up so we could begin eating. In the end we would begin anyway, and finish before he had picked up his fork. He could not be interrupted, he could not even be walked away from because he would follow, talking. I believe he enjoyed himself with us immensely. He invited us to Zürich, left parting gifts, wrote thank-you letters, and at Christmas sent an extravagant tin of Swiss cinnamon biscuits.

Mario, from Milan, brought nothing, left nothing, and said practically nothing. He arrived two days late and with a severe limp having crashed his company Porsche into a tree on the road to Milan airport. We counted ourselves lucky to have him at all, not that we lined our pockets from the £2 dinner. He dined with us rarely. When he did he would keep his napkin rolled up in its wooden ring, dab his mouth with it rolled, and return it still rolled to his sideplate. We were obtuse, we ought immediately to have given him pasta, and thereafter, but by the time we realized this, around the third day, he had abandoned our evening meal and was eating at an Italian restaurant or one of a chain of notoriously repellent fast-food palaces. He attached himself to another student at the school, Antonio, whom he brought back to us occasionally en route to fast food. Mario and Antonio took Lucy to the Tutankhamen exhibition, to a movie, and gave her a cigarette.

Mario was very young, small, and dashingly dressed: a trainee in a multi-national oil company, freshly out of university. He said the oil company was sending him to the Middle East for two years. Heaven knows how he would get on with sheep's head and palm milk when Catherine's stuffed pork tenderloin in a cheese and Madeira sauce caused him to blanch. He had never tasted fish soup and not only not tasted but never seen an avocado. We hunted in the dictionary for the Italian for avocado (it's *avocado*) but he had never heard

124

of it either. He lived with his mother who served him pasta for both lunch and supper – almost invariably spaghetti, as far as we could make out.

At least we were able to satisfy his breakfast needs, for which he wanted one small cup of sweet black coffee. That was all. Nothing to eat. We went to town on the coffee, grinding the best Brazilian high roast beans in his presence and offering a choice of white granulated, lump, or Demerera sugar. We offered a tot of brandy in the coffee but he said no. He would drink his coffee standing up or pacing round the dining-room, then flee for the Underground, handstitched topcoat flapping in the wind, doeskin briefcase swinging, Gucci shoes tip-tapping along the street.

Another Italian the school sent us was that rarity, a woman. Perhaps things are changing, have already changed, but in the seventies up-and-coming female executives were thin on the ground, and those their companies thought worth the expense of a language course virtually non-existent. Anna was twenty-three and extravagantly beautiful, though like Mario, small, a sort of shrunken-down Sophia Loren.

Apart from my not being able to take my eyes off her, Anna was a flop. She never dined with us, never had the least intention of doing so, and was never seen except when in the kitchen making pesto. She was from Genoa, home of pesto, and brought from Genoa her own basil, pine nuts, garlic, olive oil, spaghetti, and Parmesan. Anna could not be called demanding. All she asked was access to the stove and a pestle and mortar, which amazingly we had, a dinky stone-age artefact acquired from an antique shop for decoration. We offered the blender but she liked the mortar and pestle. (Question: Which is the mortar, which the pestle?) Anna ate only pesto. She made it herself, not trusting us to make it, quite rightly, and at times of her own choosing, i.e. when the kitchen was uninhabited. Whenever we arrived in the kitchen, there stood Anna pounding her ingredients to a sticky green mess. She asked if we would like her to make pesto for us. We said yes and it was smashing, our first pesto and not the last. But who would eat it to the exclusion of everything else? Man does not live by bread alone. Anna lived by pesto alone. Her gorgeousness is all I remember of Anna. Terribly unaware, brutish and male of me, I agree. Pulchritude and pesto.

Georges must be mentioned because he gave such a boost to our ego. Georges was a young bachelor in love. His field was business management, he was abroad for the first time, and everything impressed him favourably – London, Londoners, the weather, and our cooking. For Georges, all was for the best in the best of all possible worlds. Haggard from language learning, but impressed with the language school, he would appear regularly for the evening meal. Towards the end of the two weeks he paid the ultimate compliment. Finishing his wine, folding his napkin, he said, 'Me, I think you eat more good as in France.'

A French habit is to begin sentences with 'Moi, je . . .' 'Moi, j'ai faim.' 'Moi, je pense qu'il va pleuvoir.' Georges started his English sentences the same way. 'Me, I go now to bed.' We pointed out that the Me was unnecessary, and he promised he would remember, but he never did.

The telephone system profoundly impressed Georges, which was lucky because he spent a fair amount of time telephoning his bride-to-be in Paris. This was in the days before France got its telephone act very much together. 'Me, I have opinion French telephone not good,' Georges would say. 'English telephone okay.' He then talked endlessly to Paris on the kitchen telephone, punctuating his swift French with popping sounds which were kisses.

Just as well Georges did not meet Bernard, a fellow Parisian. He would have been dismayed. Bernard had only contempt for marriage and would give his reasons in grisly detail. Bernard was intellectually the brightest of our customers, none of them exactly dolts. His company was stimulating but dark. Lucy disliked him with quite remarkable fervour.

Bernard, thirty, had a string of university degrees and a wife and children whom he clearly would sooner have been without. He was in love only with bachelordom and widowerhood. He had glowering, blackguardly good looks, like Heathcliff, which must have devasted women. All right, some women. No woman in her senses would have gone near him. He would have been impossible to live with and too thrillingly dangerous for an affair. In New York he would have been in therapy or out on the streets punching people. For Bernard, all was a heap of dung in the dungiest of all possible worlds. He hated his job, something in finance that he refused to discuss, and hated the Paris quarter where he lived, and the rest of Paris. He did not regard London as an improvement. He loathed women's lib for the harm it did to women (reasons supplied), detested the English language, and reserved an especially ferocious hostility for Eva, one of the school's teachers. Every other executive who came to us worshipped Eva. He liked working with his hands, rebuilding his dilapidated house in Paris and a second hopeless house that he owned in Normandy. Choosing, surprisingly, to stay with a family rather than at a hotel, he had stipulated an informal family.

Bernard arrived informally at ten o'clock on a Saturday evening, not having been expected until the Sunday. We threw together a scratch supper of pâté, omelette, salad and cheese, which he washed down with close to a litre of red wine. For breakfast next day he appeared informally in pyjamas. On weekdays he overslept in spite of having borrowed our alarm clock. The morning I pointed out that he would be an hour late for school and Eva, he growled, 'Eva should be pleased to see me.' He would return to us with bags of grapefruit with which to start his breakfast – 'I must 'ave my vitamin C' – before proceeding to the eggs, ham, mushrooms and tomato. He drank plentifully of red wine, never complaining of its quality, and smoked Gauloises.

Angry, dishevelled Bernard demanded from Catherine her recipe for liver pâté and folded it away as if it might hold a clue to the mystery of the universe. He borrowed my raincoat on his first day and returned it on the last. Once he had owned a raincoat, he said, but his wife did not care for raincoats. (Was he in terror of his wife? She sounds as loony as him.) He had left home with an umbrella because of London's cow-pissing weather but had left it, he believed, on the plane. If we had known the location of Franthithco's umbrella vendor we could have directed Bernard thither.

Unlike Franthithco, Bernard never solicited suggestions as to what gifts he might take home. Cyanide was what we guessed he would be taking: for his family, for his colleagues in finance, for anyone who crossed his disgruntled path. He sat at the dining-room table guzzling red wine, inhaling Gauloises, and studying Lucy's copy of *Jackie*, its true experiences, make-up hints, rock celebrity page, and romantic strip cartoons. Bernard, turning the pages, would glower more and more darkly. With Gallic exuberance he explained to Lucy why what she was reading was trash. 'C'est vachement affreux,' he said in summation, spinning the offensive *Jackie* away across the table as if it were tainted offal. Lucy never forgave him. When Bernard departed in a flurry of disorganization he left behind odd, informal socks, notebooks, grapefruit, and one smouldering Lucy.

Bernard was one of very few of our paying guests who chose to stay in touch, at least for a year or two. We visited him for a day at his collapsing house in Paris, probably worth millions. His quiet wife was either cowed or a potential murderess, there was no fathoming which. A year later Bernard told us in a letter that he was divorced. We were relieved for both of them.

12 A Room with a View

CAHORS, 1979, is twelve months older and unchanged apart from sprouted parking metres. The town's official-dom is out to get cars.

Returning to the Lot was touch and go, a decision calling for a family council and show of hands. Catherine was in favour of Cahors but did not press it. I would have preferred London. A grand place, France, but at the end of the day it is only France, it isn't England. In London we would speak English and have our home back. The Venezuelan vice-consul and his relatives had long since departed, and the latest tenants, four New Zealand dentists, were about to return to Auckland and Waikokopu. They left behind in the basement stacks of skiing magazines and several damaged skis.

The girls did not appear to be passionate one way or the other until they remembered that their best friends were in Cahors. Their friends in London were two misty years in the past and growing mistier. Crucially, Kate and Polly discovered that they could not live another day without certain pungent nags, to wit, Zazie, Duke, Hector, and the impossible Bijou. Also, wait, at school they would have new teachers too, would they not? No more Madame Oeuf and Monsieur Parbleu? They eyed each other and their parents with doubt and hope.

The ayes had it.

What is changed in Cahors for us is our new flat on the top storey of a rose-red building half as old as time.

All right, the building is grey, but the tiles on the roof are a rust colour which at twilight passes for rosy. We are formidably sited at the corner of the Place Clemenceau and the rue Nationale, once the town's main thoroughfare, nowadays one-way to traffic, being too slender to cope with two cars abreast. Voyeurs, we goggle down on café life and the covered market. At this height we don't even need lace curtains. We are les enfants du paradis, watching Cahors go about its business from seats in the gods. Little escapes us. There with his ballooning biceps struts the baker. There stand two chic women in animated conversation. It's like telly with the sound off and will be as gargantuan a waste of time if we don't take care to ration ourselves. We can't hear what the chic women are saying but their hands glide, slide, stab, and flutter. The first requirement for speaking French is flexible fingers and rubber wrists. Should one of the chic women put her thumb nail under her upper incisors and flick it forward with a click, that is an insult signifying Get st-ff-d. The gesture has only been demonstrated to us, we have yet to witness it live and unrehearsed, but if we gawp through this window long enough we might.

We did not inquire if our former flat in the rue Joffre might be available. Citing fair wear and tear, the landlady chose not to refund the deposit. The Deposit is Never Refunded is a French law of life to be set alongside Nobody Hands in Anything Found on the Road, such as a mattress. May woodworm and lightning strike the rue Joffre flat and its landlady.

Gustave found us this flat. He has his ear to the ground in property matters as in other aspects of the Cahors whirligig. He visited us on Long island, his first visit to the USA, instructing his family that a history professor and politician had a responsibility to experience America first hand. He may have found Catherine a part-time teaching job at the Lycée Technique d'Agriculture, whatever that may be, but it is still to be confirmed.

Jeffrey Stride turned up on Long Island too, hauling a portfolio of paintings for the delectation of New York gallery owners; optimistically, in our opinion, his paintings being far too good. He departed with a promise of gallery space in a group exhibition next spring. Taking his paintings out of France, then bringing them back, he ran into customs trouble. Where did you acquire these paintings, Monsieur? Where are you taking them? What is their value? Are they stolen? Are they not by our own Impressionists? This one is indisputably a Monet. I must consult with the commissaire. We have only your word, Monsieur. If you painted them, where is certificate XJ49523 in evidence? They are forgeries. You must produce a notarized attestation on form 22QV proving they are not forgeries. Where is your export licence, bill of lading, sworn deposition, studbook? These paintings will have to be impounded. The impoundment fee is eleven hundred francs. The paintings must be brought back into France. The paintings must not be brought back into France. This is a final warning. Sign here, here, here, here, and here.

Sally stayed in the Lot. Someone had to look after the children. She didn't know how lucky she was. The way Jeff tells it, negotiating French customs with paintings is undiluted Kafka. Sally paints when she has the chance. She is pregnant again.

Now being summer, not everyone is on parade to greet us. Elizabeth and Jean are on holiday in England. Pierre, Francine, and their children – the teaching Pierre, not Spooky Pierre who sets pizza on fire – are by the Atlantic. Half Cahors is on vacation. In shop windows the sign FERMETURE ANNUELLE is up. The Palais Cinéma has closed, the Quercy reopened. In July and August the town's three cinemas take it in turn to shut, reducing while never entirely eliminating the selection on offer, and still allowing plenty of opportunity for screen appearances by Gérard Depardieu. A year ago I had never heard of Gérard Depardieu. No one had. Now as we creep towards the 1980s he is in every second film to arrive in town. Soon he will be in every film. We take tea with Madame Radiguet at her country house twenty minutes away, and await news from Paris that the National Assembly is to enact a law requiring that no film be made without Gérard Depardieu.

Tourists fill the space left by absent Cadurciens: Parisians, Belgians, Dutch, British, Scandinavians, Germans. Apart from an occasional bus tour we have few Americans, Canadians, or Japanese. They are all in Paris. The tourists compare menus in restaurant windows, crowd the Pont Valentré with cameras, descend into the prehistoric caves at Cabrerets, and climb up to St Cirq-Lapopie, a spectacular restored village on a cliff high above the Lot. Campers with tents are back on the towpath by the river. We have a new postman, returned from his vacation on the Mediterranean and hardly tanned at all. 'Mauvais temps,' he growls at us, as if the weather were our fault.

In second gear we climb the serpentine miles to the Wolfes' for dinner and to meet their house guests, a retired doctor and his wife from Scotland. You need to be alert on this road, especially returning to Cahors, when you keep your foot on the brake. Traffic is light but what there is you don't see until it rounds the curve immediately ahead and pounds towards you, with luck on its own side of the road. Some drivers honk before every curve, though seldom the French, considering it cissy. Not that traffic is to be blamed for the accident that overtakes Jim and Peggy Wolfe and their Scottish guests the next day on their way to the railway station.

Their car, Jim driving, goes off the road and fetches up topsy-turvy against a tree. Fortunately the drop from the road is directly into Lot scrub and trees, not into, say, a fjord. Still, so much for catching the train to Paris and flight to Glasgow. Everyone is shaken, no one mortally, though the doctor injures his back badly enough for his next three days to be spent in a hospital bed in Cahors. Jim isn't to blame, or no more than Peggy, or whoever neglected to remove an empty wine bottle from the floor by the back seat. The oversight happens easily enough, empty bottles being frequently in transit for refilling, and if the bottle is under the seat you don't see it. This bottle had rolled under the driver's seat and jammed itself beneath the brake pedal. Ergo, no brake on a precipitous downhill curve. Probably this is not the first time, nor will it be the last, that the bottle, not the contents, is responsible for an accident.

Before the rentrée and the knuckling down to earning a living, Catherine and I pay a visit to Bert and Hilda Friedman, a London couple living fifty miles away near Agen. We met when we rented their holiday accommodation one July, prior to discovering Catus. They are a self-made, self-reliant cockney couple who, their children grown and flown, sold their printing business and emigrated with two Dachshunds to France. Here in plum and peach country they bought a couple of acres of land, built a house for themselves, learning as they went, and having done that, built a second house for renting, advertising it solely in London, the last tenants they want being complaining, fault-finding Parisians. In the decade before Mrs Thatcher took the helm, this foreshadowed a central tenet of Thatcherism, namely, the ability to stand on one's own feet. In Mrs Thatcher's book, Bert and Hilda represent the best of British, or might but for their outrageous betrayal in leaving England for France of all places.

The only other Brits in Bert and Hilda's neighbourhood are Reg and Ethel, whom we understand to be penniless and who are coming to dinner. Reg spent his working years as a minor functionary in Southern Rhodesia, leaving when it looked inevitable that the country would become independent Zimbabwe. Reg and Ethel live in a caravan so small, according to the Friedmans, that they don't invite people to visit. Whether because they are ashamed after a lifetime of spacious lodgings among the frangipani trees, or because the caravan is too tiny for anyone to find, is unclear. I have the impression that the Friedmans and Reg and Ethel are friendly but not close. If they are close they will be considerably less so before the evening is over.

The red ordinaire flows. Dinner on the patio is cold cuts and salads for a summer evening. The mosquitoes are not obnoxiously active, and in the black grass, as night falls, glow-worms wink and glimmer, the first glow-worms I have seen. Not that anything is to be seen except the glow. The chat shunts to Southern Rhodesia, Zimbabwe to be, Reg being our own live pundit *in situ*, thence to other former African colonies, expanding to India, the Empire, and the metaphysics of the Raj at large.

Reg's stand, predictably, is that the colonies were far better run under British rule than now when they are self-governing. I venture that this is demonstrably so in certain respects, but they are happier governing themselves, albeit less efficiently, so must be allowed time, and in any case there is no holding back the winds of change, the tide of history, and so forth. Well-trodden stuff. Reg, miffed, plays his I-have-lived-there-and-understand-the-natives card. Bert, pouring wine, says no one has to have lived in Southern Rhodesia to know that colonialism is a blot on humanity. Reg, bridling, cites examples of material progress under colonialism. He compares Britain's benison of schools, hospitals, roads, and Christian churches, with tales of hair-raising corruption, dictatorship, and mayhem since independence. Bert brushes this aside as irrelevant. He would like Reg to tell him if he is saying that Britain took up empire-building as an exercise in philanthropy. I have shut up. Catherine, Hilda, and Ethel, have wisely not started. Reg has become pinkish and his voice is rising. He flatly declares that only those who have lived in Southern Rhodesia, have given their lives to it, can understand, a point he has made already. We shall have tears before bedtime. 'Bert,' I inquire, 'have you had any interesting tenants lately?' Bert tells Reg that colonialism, however rationalized, is a form of rape, and unacceptable. Reg tells Bert that that is communism. Bert says that if that's communism, more power to communism. Bert is admirably relaxed, leaning back in his chair, holding his glass of wine, and leaning forward only to pour more for the rest of us. He says that whatsisname, Cecil Rhodes, the bandit who conquered and founded Rhodesia, should have been strangled at birth. Imperialism was worse than a crime, it was an insult.

Reg stands up and announces, 'I'm not listening to this. Ethel, get your coat.'

This isn't happening, it's fiction, but by whom? Kipling? Dornford Yates? Evelyn Waugh? We tut-tut, shift about in embarrassment, laugh it off, and make soothing noises. Hilda implores Reg to sit. She glares at her spouse, Bert, trouble-maker, wrecker of dinner parties, reclining in his chair with a satisfied look, indifferent whether Reg leaves or not just as long as he takes Ethel with him if he does. Reg is not to be mollified. He is wounded where it hurts, in the Empire, or at the very least, the Commonwealth. He departs, meek Ethel in tow.

Hilda rounds on insensitive Bert, the Dachshunds bark, the glow-worms glow. The evening is kaput, though not for Bert, self-made Londoner, contented immigrant to France. He has built two houses and is living the life he wants to live in a spot where he wants to live it. Having waved the imperialists goodbye, he unfurls the foil and plucks the cap off the next litre of red.

Lucy, sixteen, has advanced to the Lycée Clément Marot, a gloomy pile on the Boulevard Gambetta. Marot, born in Cahors, was a witty Renaissance rhymester at the court of Francis I when he wasn't fleeing from the court, in prison, or in exile, because of his protestant leanings. He was secretary to the king's sister, Margaret of Angoulême, whose grandson, Henry of Navarre, became Henry IV, the king who thought Paris worth a mass and about whom I raved in Chapter Six, or would have, hadn't better ravers than I already done so. The yard at the Lycée Clément Marot has a bench for tired students to sit on during récré. The bench is against a wall embedded with a mosaic of coloured, broken glass and pointed flints, so you can sit on the bench but if you lean back you stab yourself.

135

Out of class, pupils have nowhere to go but this yard. No home room or common room with magazines and ping-pong. Lycée Clément Marot and Collège Gambetta have little cohesive community spirit. No attempt is made to engender one. No morning assembly with announcements, a hymn, and congratulations to the Second XI for trouncing Figeac. You arrive at school and go straight to your classroom. No school sports teams, no school newspaper, and few if any clubs or hobbies. No school song. No 'Jolly good boating weather' or 'Forty years on growing weaker and weaker'. Kate, songstress, would love the school to have to sing the *Marseillaise* daily. 'It's such a great song, not morbid like *God Save the Queen*,' she says. Organized sports and hobbies are available in Cahors but through the town, not the schools. Weekly boarders have a hard time of it. Except for Wednesday afternoon, the half day off, they are locked in the school with nothing to do but stand about and smoke Gauloises. Smoking is allowed at Clément Marot because the pupils are all sixteen or older, but at Gambetta if they want to smoke they light up in the lavatories. Punishment for such an offence is to be kept in on Wednesday afternoon to write out endless grammar or learn poems by heart. For minor infractions in the class-room the offender may be made to stand by the teacher at the front of the class. By and large the school authorities are liberal.

Liberal to a fault in some areas, such as sports. Sports occupy one three-hour period per week. Two hours, Lucy explains, by the time you have changed and been bussed to and back from the swimming pool, gymnasium, or stadium. One of her gym teachers happens to be athletic, in winter running with the class round the track at the stadium. Liberal or lazy, the others huddle together in warm clothes, talking and smoking. One is a bleached blonde aged fifty who knits for the entire session. In the gymnasium (handball, volleyball, rope-climbing, high-jumping, at least in theory) she knits and talks to the class about her divorce. Occupied as she is with knitting and talking, she is not particularly alert to truancy, and anyone so inclined has no difficulty sneaking away and

136

staying away without her noticing. Or perhaps she notices but would positively prefer people to sneak away, ideally the entire class. Girls can skip up to three sports classes a term by pleading they have their period. Tough being a boy then! 'Boys find other excuses,' Lucy says.

Two years hence Lucy will graduate from the lycée with her baccalauréat, God willing. Meanwhile she must work for it: eight hours of philosophy classes a week, much French literature, and maths up to the last moment before the final exams. Her philosophy teacher has a reputation as a ladies' man and chess player and is given to stirring things up in class. When discussion on Descartes ('I think, therefore I am') leads somehow to spiritualism, he has the class clustered round a Ouija board. When Freud is the text he discloses that he dreamed that a female pupil in the class, name withheld, was walking naked towards him along the Boulevard Gambetta. Probably untrue but nobody is sure. Which female? Perturbation in class: whispering, pointing, vigorous head-shaking. Some parents are nervous that the still amorphous minds of their offspring be exposed to this unpredictable fellow, especially as one of the texts is Marx. (An enduring phenomenon at times of national elections is a provincial left-wing vote known as the lycée professors' vote.) Another text, predictably, is Sartre. A few years on, Lucy's philosophy professor at London University, an American, will inform her that Sartre is not a philosopher but a pamphleteer, a French gadfly. Her philosophy homework is to write an essay, Do Values Exist? She receives fourteen out of twenty and is well pleased with herself.

Kate, twelve, has problems with Latin so I send off to London for *Kennedy's Latin Primer*, if it still exists. Probably it does. It existed for a millenium before it was handed out to my generation. Mr Kennedy and his heirs must be billionaires. The *Primer* arrives and Kate and I buckle down. *Hic haec hoc.* We don't make much headway. For progress to show in class and homework Kate's Latin really needs to be learned in French. The lessons are quietly dropped, the *Primer* goes on the reference shelf. Kate maturely suffers

Latin and its elderly teacher, waiting them out. She'd make a splendid Quaker, going limp at non-violent demonstrations and allowing herself to be manhandled into the police wagon. She realizes that the day will come when her trials over Latin will end for ever, terminally cut off like an aristocrat's head in the Revolution.

Polly arrives home with art homework. This is promising, the first time art has featured in her syllabus. She seems to have done much of the drawing already, a landscape with a tree in the foreground, a house, horizon, and sky, in tricky *encre de Chine*, China ink. Most of the drawing consists of diagonally ruled lines. She didn't make it up – everyone in the class does the same drawing, she tells us. We might have guessed. Still, even Renoir had to start somewhere, and it might have been aged ten with lots of ruled lines. I lend a hand in completing the landscape and the result isn't bad. I have a modest talent for drawings of the dashed-off school. Polly returns from her next art class with the same drawing and fresh paper. The art master had said her work was poor and must be done again. It's to do with perspective, Polly says wonderingly. This news is unwelcome. Perspective I was never great shakes at, holding the pencil at arm's length, closing one eye, sliding your thumb up and down the pencil. All I ever saw was my thumb and the pencil. But I offer assistance, if she would like, and together we accomplish a minor masterpiece less smudged than the first. Renoir, move over. Polly brings it home to do a third time. The shading is wrong, these lines are too diagonal, those not diagonal enough. My opinion is that her art master is a pedant and a sadist. He probably has a waxed moustache and a goatee. Certainly he is anti-British. 'You must hate him,' I say. 'I quite like him,' Polly says. We execute a landscape of flawless diagonals and blistering perspective. I add a bunny rabbit, alert by the base of the tree. The rabbit is more Chagall than Renoir and has an unexpected cubist touch, but it is identifiably a rabbit, or some kind of beast. Polly is unsure about the rabbit. She has reason. The teacher awards the drawing four out of twenty and tells Polly she is très frivole.

Worse is to come. Homework for Polly's French class is to write a story about a pet. She may choose the pet but the story should start with a newspaper advertisement for a pet, that she has either inserted or responds to. What pet are you choosing? we ask. Polly supposes a cat or a dog. 'Boring!' exclaims Catherine. 'Everybody will be writing about cats and dogs!' An alligator is agreed on. Polly hops away to see what *Larousse* has to say about alligators. She writes about a man alligator living in a bathtub who sees in a newspaper an advertisement from a lady alligator. This results in the two alligators getting together. The essay receives zero.

Catherine is furious. She telephones the teacher, Madame Maurois, and arranges for an appointment at the school. Madame Maurois keeps Catherine waiting half an hour. She has blonde pigtails and is putting on her fur coat when Catherine, at last admitted, zooms in – I'd not relish having been in Madame's fur coat – and challenges the zero mark.

Madame Maurois says the essay had many errors. Catherine says that it didn't have a zero-grade number of errors. Madame says an alligator is not a pet, she will not accept an alligator. Catherine says people do indeed have alligators as pets. Madame says no they don't. Catherine demands to know if she would accept, say, a goldfish? Yes, Madame would accept a goldfish. Would she accept a goat? After reflection, yes, Madame would accept a goat. If, Catherine argues, closing for the kill, a smelly goat, why not an alligator? Didn't Madame think the choice of an alligator at least showed some imagination? 'When I want imagination, I shall ask for it,' Madame says.

Collapse of Catherine. The mark remains zero.

At the top of the stairs is the room where I sit, there isn't any other room quite like it.

The room is a vast attic choc-a-bloc with foulness and wreckage, broken furniture, split cabin trunks, strewn rubble, infested, ruined clothing, and piles of rancid, yellowing women's magazines, possibly of specialist interest, even of value, if they could be rid of worm and rot. The only mention the landlord makes of this hideous limbo is that we must ignore it, one day he will have it cleared. This is either a barefaced lie – he is too lazy to clear it himself and too miserly to pay anyone – or wishful thinking of majestic proportions. The only way to clear the attic would be to blow up the building. Here I have cleared a space not directly beneath a cobwebbed skylight – cobwebs are all that holds the skylight in place – swept aside the powdery bones of slaughtered Albigensian heretics, and set up my table, chair, and typewriter. My work room is not the glassed-in study which Victor Hugo in exile built at the top of his house in Guernsey, where he wrote standing up and on a clear day could see the French coast, neither is it Bernard Shaw's revolving summer house, but external trappings are neither here nor there in the creation of ineffable literature. It's the inner fire. Talking of fire, I don't expect to be here much in the winter. The attic has no heat, light, or sockets to make either possible. On occasion, on a roll, out of earshot of the Rolling Stones in the living quarters below, I light a candle. This is so unbearably glamorous – am I Chaucer? Chatterton? The Venerable Bede? – that I cannot concentrate. If I look up I see slices of twilit sky through the gaps in the rose-red tiles. One puff of wind through those tiles and my guttering candle could be among the women's magazines. Forget inner fire. I envisage a conflagration that will clear the landlord's attic for him before the pompiers with their hoses have *pam-pom pam-pommed* into position in the Place Clemenceau.

Halfway up the stairs is Kate's little room, the clearing of which requires more than a broom.

The master's study is a gigantic garbage-filled tundra. Kate, by request, has a garbage-filled cupboard between the flat and the attic. We were unaware of its existence for two months, the door being curved and part of the spiralling wall. A keyhole is the giveaway but unless you are looking for it you don't notice it. The door and the entire wall's brick and plaster from street to attic are ravaged by what can only have been regular assaults up and down the stairway by a brigade of the Gendarmerie Nationale in képis firing their pistols. The contents of Kate's coveted (by her) cupboard are plainly an overflow from the garret above, so we shift the refuse back, sweep, and scrub. What remains is a cupboard with space for a mattress, card table, and kitchen chair. We leave a leaning shelf holding beetle-encrusted volumes of *Angélique*, a romantic novel, Kate will one day explain to us, that she devours from start to finish, more than once feigning illness so as to be excused school. Shutting herself in her closet, an Emma Bovary in the making, Kate swoons over *Angélique*. Gustave, in his electrician's hat, rigs up terrifying yet effective electricals which provide sporadic heat and light, though if Kate turns on her heater while someone happens to be ironing below, we are plunged into darkness. Into her boudoir Kate smuggles a secret mouse. We have banned pets because of droppings and dysentery, and what if the beast should chew through one of Gustave's electrical connections? We could lose Kate, the upper reaches of the building, perhaps part of the medieval quarter of Cahors. Kate feeds her mouse on chocolate, we later learn, reads *Angélique*, invites her friends in, and descends for meals, school, and trips to the stables to ride Hector and the terrible Bijou. In time these trips will be made aboard a second-hand Mobilette, a sort of light motorcycle or scooter without gears which she receives before her fourteenth birthday because she can't wait. Fourteen is the legal age for conducting such a machine along the public highways, so until then it is stored in the master's aerie. Here, when the master is not at his desk, Kate sits astride her scooter, starts it up, and pretends she is scootering along the Boulevard Gambetta, waving as she goes to poor scooterless pedestrians.

The mouse, meanwhile, has died of chocolate poisoning.

13 Black Wine of Cahors

CATHERINE IS packing work clothes and warm jerseys preparatory to departing to a hilltop vineyard fifteen kilometres away for the *vendanges*: the grape harvest. She will return only for the briefest of weekends, her boss evidently being a slave-driver, a Simon Legree of the Lot, who works his team an eight-hour day and releases them only from noon on Saturday to sunrise on Monday. Monsieur Buzot turns out to be more jovial than Simon Legree but he permits no shilly-shallying. The grapes must be got in. For three weeks the girls will be motherless, surviving on their own cooking (pancakes) and their father's (crapaud-en-trou Yorkshire – toad-in-the-hole).

Should she take a pillow? If her bed has one of the bolsters the French are so fond of, an unmanoeuverable log trapped beneath a sheet, she'll not sleep a wink.

For plunging into experiences which would leave some of us whimpering with anxiety, few there are to compare with an intrepid breed of Anglo-Irish (father's side) and Canadian pioneering spirit (mother's side). A couple of summers hence Catherine will embark from Paris on a car rally across the Sahara to Timbuktu. She won't quite make it to Timbuktu. Not many will. The bones of her Volkswagen Beetle will be left to bleach in the desert sands. But the attempt will have been made. In Victorian times Cath might have been found on the Zambezi wearing ankle-length skirts, reprimanding the bearers for sloth, and carrying a parasol and cannisters of Twining's tea. To the grape harvest she is taking Lipton's teabags, aware that for breakfast the choice will be coffee, chocolate, and wine, but no tea. She packs her French dictionary and for the evenings a skirt and perfume.

She doubts there'll be cocktail parties and dancing in the evening. This is grape picking, not a cruise ship. But best to be prepared. The grape harvest is after all a celebration of Bacchus, a time of merriment and over-indulgence. Rumour has it one eats well. Polly picks from the Happy Families pack the card of Mrs Bunn, the baker's wife, a fat, squat shrew of a woman. She says, 'You won't end up like that, will you?'

She might not if the picking is as gruelling as people insist it is. Long hours, backache, and a risk of snipped fingers. Hearing that she is off to the *vendanges*, friends grimace in incredulity and clutch their backs and totter. We shall see. Or rather Catherine will.

To be sure we can find the vineyard we make an exploratory sortie. We wind upward from the poplar-lined river Lot into mist like wool on the hills, and mounting higher, pierce the wool like an aeroplane breaking through cloud cover. The hamlet is sprayed in sunshine. Swallows dive-bomb the dozen houses, church, and school. Ducks, geese and chickens peck in the streets, if streets is the word for the lumpy spaces between the houses. Dogs snooze and scrounge. Beyond the hamlet the vineyard reaches away across the plateau, ripe for picking.

The church, with a new bell tower as sturdy as Mrs Bunn, is kept locked except for the infrequent occasions when the priest arrives from the valley to conduct a service. There had been a time when the church stayed open, but revellers who had harvested the grape all day and drunk its product all evening once entered and garlanded it with paper streamers. Now the priest keeps it locked to saints and sinners alike. The school too is closed. The hamlet's few children board a bus each day for a school in the valley. This is the depopulated Lot which in the fifty years up to 1920 lost one in every two inhabitants. The limestone houses have an outside stairway up to a balcony and the first floor where the rooms are. At ground level is the cellar for storing wine, preserved goose, and walnuts. The only concession to frivolity is the roof of curved red tiles, as if an ailing, whey-faced person had put a wavy red wig on his head to cheer things up. Above some roofs towers a pigeonnier with openings at the top for pigeons to come and go. In the past pigeon-droppings had such value as a fertilizer that when the master of the house died the droppings were divided among his heirs.

At the far end of the hamlet stands the house of Monsieur and Madame Buzot. They are at home and welcoming, though Monsieur is sorry but in two minutes he must be off to the vineyard. She is short and stocky, he is pretty huge by Lot standards. He towers above his new recruit to the harvest, who is five feet eight. As a result of a sequence of profitable *vendanges* their house has sprouted an east wing, the terrace has been extended, and every inch of wall is busy with pots of geraniums. Madame painted the pots, taking weeks over the task. Behind the terrace are bedrooms and a new bathroom. Below are new garages for the car and tractor. Slave quarters have been constructed especially for the *vendanges*. We are shown a luxurious room (not in the slave quarters) with a mantelpiece on which sit dolls in gaudy crocheted dresses. Hand-made antimacassars drape the chairs. Dominating all is a colossal TV screen. Monsieur Buzot relates how his extension has aroused such envy in the neighbourhood that he has lost one of his oldest friends. This friend had previously called in every day to chat and drink wine. Since the building of the extension he has not only stopped visiting but can hardly bring himself to say Bonjour on chance meetings.

Around the house are vegetable and flower gardens and fruit trees. All the vegetables the grape-pickers will eat are fresh from the garden except wild mushrooms from the woods and occasional tinned peas, which the French claim upset the liver but eat anyway. Punctuating the gardens are sheds, rabbit hutches, vats for the wine, and a stable for a cart-horse. The horse's sole function is to turn the soil between the older rows of vines that were planted too close for a tractor to pass between. This task he performs twice a year. The rest of the year he leads the life of Riley in a buttercup field or being groomed in the stable.

You could lose Kate's room in one of these wine vats. Monsieur Buzot, as a young man, built them during the war, trading a sack of potatoes for each bag of cement. Oxen hauled the cement up from the valley. On one vat is a rendering in relief of the Pont Valentré.

He rinses glasses under a tap and fills them from a vat. It's a little early in the day, and I wish I could understand what he is saying because it is obviously instructive and he is saying a great deal. Is the wine routine Buzot ordinaire or could it be vin de Cahors, the wine Peter the Great drank to cure his stomach ulcer, and the father of Grand Master Anatoly Karpov chose to calm his fevers, according to *Karpov on Karpov: Memoirs of a Chess World Champion*? I catch technical terms like *cuve* (vat), *degré alcoolique* (alcoholic strength), and *tanin* (tannin). If I knew what I was tasting I would have a better idea how enthusiastic to be.

The wine is so cold it tastes of nothing. Does Monsieur Buzot not know that red wine should be drunk at room temperature? I am not going to be the one to tell him. True, the wine is in a room, but it is a room that is not much more than a roof, and last night the temperature was only just above freezing. There is no receptacle for spitting the wine into either, as there would be in a correctly-run tasting, not that the floor will suffer, being of compacted earth. Catherine and I enter into the ritual sighing and eye-rolling over the wine's nose and legs. Heated up it probably wouldn't be at all bad. Monsieur Buzot beams, tosses back the contents of his glass, and says something to the effect that it is bon, ce vin, eh? Vin he pronounces veng.

A little history. Every locality in France has its speciality for the table, the speciality has its history, and there is no easeful living in the locality while in ignorance of the speciality and its history. The speciality confronts you in numberless shop windows and is constantly discussed. As a guest you will be served it with a flourish, and if you don't know what it is the next hour will pass hearing it explained to you. Best to discover right away what you can about the speciality and be done with it. The proudest speciality of Cahors is Vin de Cahors.

The grapes Catherine will be picking are Auxerrois, for the most part, and the end product will be Vin de Cahors, or the juice of the first fermentation will be. What is left, the vin de presse, will be respectable ordinaire. Cahors wine is rich in tannin, an organic substance found in a variety of plants (tea, coffee, walnuts, mangrove, hemlock), and used to make ink and dye, to tan leather, and to treat burns. This may not sound a promising ingredient for wine but tannin's main effect seems to be on the wine's colour. Cahors wine is a deep dark red. Edward III dubbed it 'the black wine of Cahors'.

Describing a wine in words is an unrewarding exercise. Step over a fine line and you are a target for a raspberry. Remember the gentleman in the Thurber cartoon? 'It's a naive domestic Burgundy without any breeding, but I think you'll be amused by its presumption.'

Here goes anyway. Fools rush in. A good Cahors wine is round, astringent, distinctive, easy to drink, and thoroughly agreeable.

A wine connoisseur we meet – not that everyone here isn't a wine connoisseur – tells us that Cahors wine can't be compared with any other wine because it is utterly itself, unlike any other. It has the *goût de terroir*, the taste of the locality, *terroir* in this context meaning more than mere soil but the tradition and aesthetic of the region. 'After swallowing some of our best Cahors,' he says, 'I've counted up to twenty before the taste is gone. That's rare. Even with most of the big Bordeaux wines the taste disappears after a count of ten or twelve.'

Epic poets and film producers in search of a subject might look further and fare worse than the saga of Vin de Cahors, throbbing as it is with romance, cosmic catastrophe, human endeavour, topicality, and with a happy ending thrown in. Annual production in 1816, the year after Waterloo, 175,000 barrels. Production in 1958, 650 barrels, and a real possibility that soon there would be no more ever, amen. Vin de Cahors wiped from Planet Earth. I like to think it is Catherine's demon picking that turns the tide. The truth is that by the early 1980s the renaissance has been under way for twenty years, not that that's particularly long for a wine two thousand years old.

The Romans brought the first vines to Quercy, where no sooner had viticulture got under way than it almost ended. In AD 92 the Emperor Domitian (murdered in a palace conspiracy led by his wife) ordered the destruction of half the provincial vineyards to make room for grain. The vines of Quercy remained uprooted for two centuries until replanting began under a wine enthusiast, the Emperor Probus (murdered by his troops). The quality of the new vines was good. In the seventh century the Bishop of Verdun was writing effusive thanks to the Bishop of Cahors for a gift of 'dix vases du noble Falerne'. The comparison of Cahors wine with Falernian, the wine of south Italy praised by Horace and Virgil, was as high as tributes come. By 1225 Vin de Cahors was being quoted on the London market.

Pope John XXII, the financier, gave the wine of his native Quercy a boost by ordering the Auxerrois vines cultivated there to be planted at the papal palace at Avignon. After the papal palace, the royal palace at Fontainebleau, where another two hundred years on Francis I commanded the planting of an arbour of Auxerrois vines. The problem wasn't producing stunning wine but distributing it. Once the wine reached Bordeaux it could be shipped anywhere by sea, but to arrive there the barges had to navigate the frequently treacherous Lot. Tons of wine and grain went to the bottom of the river each year. Once the wine was in Bordeaux, the world's greatest single vineyard, the jealous Bordelais slapped crippling duties on it and often would not allow it out of the port.

The wine got around and its reputation waxed anyway. The

privileged drank it at banquets aboard French transport ships while the lower orders made do with Vin de Graves and Vin de Bordeaux. The wine went in bulk to England and northern Europe. In Russia, Caorskoie Vino became the ceremonial wine at mass in the Russian Orthodox Church. Vin de Cahors reached the American colonies where fraud discredited it, cochineal being added to rubbish wine for colouring and the result sold as finest imported Vin de Cahors. The half century following the Napoleonic Wars became a golden age of Cahors wine, as for all French wines.

What went wrong? Why, come the 1950s, was the end nigh for Vin de Cahors?

One reason was competition from the new vineyards of the Midi, that vast area of southern France reaching from the Spanish border to the Rhône. With few exceptions these Languedoc wines were not up to the standard of Cahors wine, but with the railway they could travel fast and in bulk to all parts of France. They took business away from all the old established vineyards, and while the great estates of Bordeaux and Burgundy could weather the competition, small growers of wines such as Vin de Cahors suffered.

The second reason, familiar to all wine buffs, was a vine louse first recorded in 1863 at Kew, in London, in imported American vines. Two years later decay was noticed in France, near Tarascon, where a nurseryman was selling vines resistant to vine mildew. The next year the same infection appeared at Floirac in the Gironde. In 1868 the louse became known as phylloxera.

Wine history divides itself into pre-phylloxera and post-phylloxera. In teeming colonies the vine louse ate the roots of the vines, reaching Quercy in 1877 and destroying half the vineyards. By the end of the decade most of the Bordeaux vineyards were devastated, and a few years later those of Champagne and Burgundy. Two-and-a-half million acres of French vines were laid waste.

The solution was eventually found to be the grafting of French vines – what was left of them – onto imported, louse-resistant American vines. From America came both louse and remedy. The graftings were in general a success, but in the Lot entire tracts of land had been abandoned, the farmers and their families having lost heart and boarded trains for Paris and boats for the colonies. Two more American diseases struck, black rot and mildew, and returned again and again to wreck the grape harvests. For the Lot the coup de grâce was Algerian wine, deluging the country from 1930, and all right for mixing with the rough stuff of the Midi but not with Vin de Cahors. Rarely if ever has a quality wine been so overwhelmed with disaster. Twenty years ago these grapes in Monsieur Buzot's vineyard had all but vanished from the Lot.

How come the resurrection? Zoom, pan, close-up, long-shot, and music up on scenes of grafting experiments, studies of soil and climate, grinding work in vineyards, the founding of a co-operative, and the dedication of farmers such as José Baudel, head of the co-operative. (Gérard Depardieu will play José Baudel.) The award in 1970 of the official stamp of approval, Appellation d'Origine Contrôlée, has done no harm either. In the last ten years production of Vin de Cahors has trebled.

We drive from Monsieur Buzot's vineyard back to Cahors by way of the *caves* co-operative at Parnac beside the Lot. In the sunny yard customers are presenting *bonbonnes* of varying capacity and design for filling up with ordinaire. A *bonbonne* is a container for wine and the procedure could hardly be less romantic, being like nothing so much as having your car tanked up with premium unleaded. So much for the blushful Hippocrene with beaded bubbles winking at the brim. An attendant, who might be a typist summoned from the office, or a child, inserts the nozzle of a hose into the *bonbonne*'s neck and in foams the plonk. If you don't have a *bonbonne* the co-operative will sell you an inflatable plastic one with a screw-on cap, as banal as the filling by hosepipe, but cheap, and the wine tastes the same. Traditional, pricier *bonbonnes* are of glass encased in sturdy wicker, or in raffia, the whiskery stuff round the Chianti bottles which once upon a time were a lamp in every student's digs. These *bonbonnes* have a cork. In hardware stores, near the nails, screws, staples, flanges, and grommets, are tray upon tray of every size of cork.

Beyond the vin ordinaire hosepipes, at a counter in a shed huge as an aeroplane hangar, stand customers tasting the vrai Vin de Cahors. They sniff, swirl, sip, swill, rinse, either spit or swallow, smile, frown, and ask next to taste the vrai Vieux Cahors, vintage of sixty-seven or whatever. In time they settle for a case of this, or a lone bottle of that, or they slink away buying nothing, obvious freeloaders. This is the *salle de dégustation*, the room where you taste.

DEGUSTATION proclaim billboards along the routes of France. No matter how often I see the sign, I feel queasy, the word *dégustation* suggesting something to be avoided, a mixture of disgust and indigestion.

At a counter a burly fellow swallows Vin de Cahors, pauses, closes his eyes, makes cooing sounds, and says sacrilegiously, 'C'est le sang de Jésus!'

Certainly not an Englishman. A Parisian? Presumably he is a local, a Lotois, a Cadurcien even, they being the most given to praise for Cahors wine. This is normal. The Bordelais eulogise their Bordeaux wine, Normans laud cider and Calvados, and Scots their single malt.

Good Cahors wine is sumptuous, no denying it. So it always comes as a surprise to us when a Cahors native observes that it's not so sumptuous, not particularly to his palate, not the most luscious wine ever, that indeed – whisper it low – the people of the Lot overpraise it. Remember that *goût de terroir*, that indefinable flavour of the region? André Simon, food and wine writer, was sceptical about *goût de terroir*, considering it 'a somewhat assertive quality, usually highly appreciated locally, where the wine is made, but not so much to the taste of the unbiased'.

Enough dilly-dallying. I must get Catherine back to the flat so that she may do press-ups and back-strengthening exercises in readiness for this immemorial, positively Biblical event where 'they shall sit every man under his vine and under

150

his fig tree' (Micah 4:4), except that any man sitting under Monsieur Buzot's vines, woman too, instead of going snip, snip, snip in a frenzy of picking, is likely to bring down the Gallic wrath of Monsieur, who weighs in at around 250 pounds.

14 Backache and Blood

H ERE THEN the epic tale of a Lot *vendanges*, received in despatches from Corporal Catherine, GP (Grape Picker), in the front line, and decoded by the Brigadier and his staff at GHQ, Place Clemenceau, Cahors. No lives are lost in the engagement, yet is blood spilled, which is normal when amateurs are picking, as we shall see.

First the harvest meals, this being the point of the exercise for many pickers, especially those weak in commitment to work; next a glimpse of the bereft Brigadier and staff behind the lines; then the pickers themselves, scarred veterans and green recruits, and how you pick. I have picked in France and the United States and there is not much difference. What difference there is isn't cultural – wherever you pick, the boss wants the grapes in fast – but botanical. Height of the bunches of grapes from the ground, stalk thickness, that sort of thing.

Wherever the vineyard, you are not paid much, but you don't starve.

When the farmhouse belonged to Madame Buzot's father it had no sanitation and the family lived in the kitchen. Now that it is a show house with sensational plumbing, and Monsieur Buzot's pal spurns him out of envy, the pickers still live in the kitchen when they're not picking or sleeping. But the kitchen has changed and is Madame's pride. She has an electric carving knife, electric clock, electric tin-opener, electric coffee grinder, electric rôtisserie, electric dishwasher, electric clothes washer, and electric stove. It is still a traditional French kitchen – oilcloth on the table, dogs trooping in and out – but camouflaged by a sparkling contemporary look. In this kitchen, for three weeks, the dozen harvesters tackle the famous, infamous grape-harvest gourmandise.

Madame knows how to cook. We may picture, in attendance, slicing and stirring, sisters, nieces, and aunts – no males – but Madame is queen. Each course is an art. Not three-star Michelin art, not cuisine minceur art either, but grape-harvest art for toilers in the vineyards of the Lord, the Lord being Monsieur Buzot, seated at the head of the table. Lunch is five courses starting with a thick country soup: broad beans, green beans, potatoes, lumps of bread. This is a meal in itself and the one course Catherine isn't wild about, not least because if you do it justice you have little room left for whatever is to follow. After the soup, garden vegetables, perhaps green beans cooked in meat juices with many lurking garlic cloves, or a tomato salad dressed with onion rings, parsley, and vinaigrette, or radishes with their green stalks on and eaten with butter, bread, and salt. Next, eggs in mayonnaise, or a cold rice salad, or macaroni and cheese, or potatoes in one form or another, a course stiff with carbos, but you can't say no thank you, Madame watches everyone's every forkful. To say no would be an insult and it is all so good anyway. Then the meat. Because Monsieur and Madame keep rabbits this course is frequently rabbit. One lunch it is a civet, a stew with a gamey wine sauce, Catherine's favourite of the three weeks' feasting. At other lunches arrive lamb, beef, pork, or chicken. Never fish. There is perpetual house red, which is to say, this house's red, Monsieur Buzot's own, what else? Unusual for here, the Lot, Madame is not interested in dessert tarts and cakes, but there is cheese.

The evening meal includes an additional dish, often pâté or saucisson. By evening the troops have laboured all day so they need a little extra.

Madame has arms like rolled-up eiderdowns. For most of the meal she is completing preparations for the next course, then serving everybody. She sits and swallows some food before springing up as in a game of musical chairs to prepare and serve once more. No one at the table pays much attention to the wants of others. The moment food hits the table the troops fall on it. No question of waiting till all are served.

This regimen makes Madame's life in the kitchen hectic, but she has chosen to have it that way, and presumably she is enjoying herself, not that you would guess it from her expression, which is dour, crinkling into a semblance of satisfaction only when someone takes a moment to exclaim, 'Mais c'est bieng, le civet!' and 'Felicitations, Madame!' and 'Formidable!' The each-for-himself approach means that no sooner has one customer started to eat than another has finished. The advantage is that you eat your food while it is hot. At the Jacobean refectory table in the crumbling Irish Deanery where Catherine grew up, your mutton, roast spuds, Brussels sprouts, and gravy, might cool and congeal on your plate before the entire company was served and you picked up your Queen Anne knife and fork.

Men have priority. Everyone is provided with a fork, glass, and soup bowl, the bowl serving for the entire meal and the glass for all liquids including coffee. No side plates. In France none but the poshest offer a side plate. Some receive a knife but the men who have attended the harvest before conjure from a pocket a chunky boy-scout knife with blades, corkscrews, and horse-hoof picks. They open a blade and use it as their knife, demonstrating membership of the in-group. There being no breadboard, Madame cradles a loaf the size of a small car tyre against the shelf of her bosom and with an ordinary sharp knife slices perilously inward, wedge after wedge. In the Lot, or anywhere in France, we have rarely seen a breadboard or a bread knife.

After the flow of the house red and the coffee, an inch of ratafia might be poured into the glass. This is the home-made brew that Monsieur Becquet in Catus used to give us, a killer liqueur of white grape juice mixed with marc, the fiery distillation of the pith, pips, skins, and stalks of the crushed grapes. Marc on its own is so foul you have to mix something into it. Occasionally, when he feels like it, Monsieur Buzot uncorks a bottle of champagne. This he does deftly, just the soft burp of the cork and a trickle of smoke. Unless you are watching you miss it. No theatrics, no exploding cork, spouting foam, maniacal yell, and certainly no hosing the stuff over people's heads like a Grand Prix winner. No one need fear for his eye when Monsieur Buzot opens champagne.

I once knew a Belgian girl, name of Claire, whose father had lost an eye to a champagne cork, an injury less uncommon among champagne drinkers than might be supposed. On the neck label of American champagne and fizzy wine is the warning: *Warning! Be careful! Point bottle away from self and others! Do not shake! Never use a cork remover!* What you do, says the label, is twist stopper out slowly by hand. My experience is that some stoppers won't twist, the bottle needs a bit of a shake. When that doesn't work either, you put on a flattering grin and hand the bottle to a macho toper who can't refuse. Then you flee and cover your eyes. Somewhere I read that it is important to twist the bottle, not the cork, or was it the cork you twist, not the bottle?

Anyway, Monsieur Buzot opens the champers with no more fuss than if he were opening a letter. The French seem to bring out champagne at the end of a meal when all that normal people can do is lie down and twitch. With it come cloyingly sweet supermarket biscuits. These are pretty much the extent of Madame Buzot's interest in dessert. Given what has gone before, I would feel the same. With the champagne at one harvest lunchtime the troops attain the height of children's party treats when they are presented with a chocolate ice cream on a stick.

At GHQ we can't compete with this kind of cuisine. What we can do, once anyway, is eat out. We are entitled. The chef is absent, gorging herself like Henry VIII.

155

We seldom eat in restaurants. This perhaps makes a small nonsense of our living in France. But in restaurants the girls grow restless, sitting for ever while food comes and goes with nothing to do but eat. For a family of five the bill adds up, especially when we all want the priciest items, such as the goose confit. French restaurant lamb is raw. The only time we ordered lamb (in transit, somewhere in mid-France) we steeled ourselves, sweating from our temerity, to ask if the lamb could go back and have heat applied. The waitress blanched, gathered up the lamb, and treated us like grubs for the rest of the meal. She may have been the cook's wife. Dawn was on its way before she came back with the lamb, still raw.

We have also had stunning restaurant meals, decent anyway, nothing mentioned in *Michelin* yet, but one day. Tonight's will be at least okay, if it kills me. The treat is for me, fast fading from trying to dream up an evening meal that will be acceptable to all and not recycled from the previous evening, and the evening before that.

Polly, thrilled at the prospect of an evening out, just like an adult, leads me on an exhaustive survey of the menus posted in the town's restaurant windows. She knows far more about the highways and byways of Cahors than I do. We jaunt up one side of the Boulevard Gambetta, down the other, to the railway station, and return to our Place Clemenceau by way of the Pont Valentré.

Whatever else, Polly insists, there must be chips.

Fine with me. France's lamb may be raw, and the beef not much better, but the french fries are usually bliss. I will not make chips at home because the one time I tried the pan caught fire. The girls vanished under the table. With considerable presence of mind, also bravery, I carried the blaze outdoors where in time it died. Any alternative, such as blowing on it, would have led to the flashing lights and wha-wha-wha-wha of the pompiers.

We settle for a restaurant on the Place Clemenceau, fifteen yards from our flat, and enter with our hands washed and hearts high, if not palpitating. The most modest menu, a menu to break nobody's bank, includes pommes frites, wine, and service. The restaurant is cavernous, unadorned, and empty apart from a group at the bar and three or four diners at tables close to the television. The girls hurtle to the unoccupied table closest to the television and seat themselves facing the screen. A child-daughter of the proprietor arrives with a menu. When I request the least pricey set meal for four – no need to study the à la carte: all we want is chips – she recovers the menu and departs. Immediately she is back with a basket of bread, a litre of vin rouge, and a tureen of the same vegetable soup which the girls reject at school every lunchtime. We have lighted on a no-nonsense restaurant.

Lucy, Kate, and Polly refuse the soup and watch the TV screen. The soup has its predictable floating slices of yesteryear's bread and is not at all bad. Somebody has to eat it. The next course is a slightly more popular hors d'oeuvre of vinegary beets, radishes, rice and ham, which the girls pick at, then turn their backs on. The hors d'oeuvre evokes memories of the salad bar at London's big Lyons Corner Houses in the forties and fifties: miles of gaudy salads you helped yourself to, all tasting of vinegar. Chewing bread, L, K, and P watch in silence the TV's Hollywood movie.

For the main course the child waitress, speaking for the first time, offers a choice of steak, veal, or lamb. An assortment is agreed on, including lamb. Who knows, it might be overcooked and merely pink. The flesh arrives promptly, accompanied by a replenished basket of bread and a smoking hill of chips. It is an hour or more since we sat down, and the girls are full of bread, but now they face the food, and the chip hill vanishes, as does the meat. Half a litre of wine also seems to have vanished, which can't be blamed on the girls, who have gaseous fruit juices. The wine isn't even particularly pleasant, indeed it is somewhat sour, prickly, as if the carafe had been filled by sinking it into an open vat in a yard behind the restaurant. My major error is admitting having seen, years ago, the film on the screen. It is *Klute*, with Jane Fonda and Donald Sutherland, dubbed into French. From now on I am expected to give Kate and Polly a running commentary on the plot, of which I remember little, not even who are the goodies, who the baddies.

Cheese follows, and packaged ice cream, which is as much a triumph as were the chips. Each course has been exactly as expected. We have been two hours at the table, and sleep is winning, even over the imminent conclusion of *Klute*. We tack into the night, back to the Place Clemenceau and bed.

By and large a successful dinner, though the conversation had hardly sparkled.

Meanwhile, back at the front, Monsieur Buzot wakes up the pickers each morning by striding through the slave quarters, rapping on each door, and shouting, 'Au boulot!' To the grindstone! On the kitchen table are soup, cold sausage, pâté, ham, bread, butter, and coffee. The men drain their soup, pour red wine into the bowl, swirl it, and drink it down. Some round off breakfast with a half glass of marc.

Catherine is able to face little of this but she has her teabags. Madame offers to make the tea for her. Catherine accepts. She hasn't a lot of choice. Madame is not one to brook interference in her kitchen, somebody messing about at her stove, particularly a foreigner. After a day or two Catherine is wondering why the tea has become undrinkable. Only after the end of the first week does she discover that Madame is using the same teabag over and over. Whether from frugality or ignorance is unknown.

The pickers number ten or twelve, depending on the dropping in of one or two non-resident irregulars. Two are retired men, both wearing *bleus*, the blue denim overalls for farm work. Jean is a blue-eyed Breton who looks fifty but is ten years older. He is retired from the railways and happy breeding rabbits, playing cards, improving his house in Brittany, gardening, and taking his beloved dog for walks. He has brought innumerable photographs of the dog, a very ordinary-looking dog, and is for ever showing them round. He's not an expert photographer. Sometimes the view is of the dog's hindquarters, sometimes a leg, sometimes a close-up of part of the head. Catherine sees photos of the dog in front of the Brittany house, behind the house, walking towards it, away from it, sleeping, begging, eating, and sitting doing nothing, perhaps thinking please, enough photographs already. Jean teases Catherine all day long, often with ribaldry you would not find in the best drawing-rooms, but she likes him. He's a softy. Each year he escapes from his wife, he says, by coming here for the *vendanges*. Each year his wife sends him off with an envelope stamped and addressed to herself and one sheet of paper. All she asks is two lines saying he has arrived and is well. He never manages to get the letter off. It stays in his suitcase and returns blankly home with him at the end of the harvest.

André, the other retired worker, is from here, the Lot, and brims with old wives' tales. Having your back to a TV that is switched on will give you a headache. Garlic and onion are good for the circulation (he might be right on that). You will get a headache from wearing gumboots indoors. Each mealtime André helps himself to spoonfuls of garlic cloves, digging them out from the meat and vegetables. He is arthritic but he works away among the vines without complaining.

Among the others is a university student from Toulouse, a Gallic gallant, a Cyrano, who each morning before work runs out and picks Catherine a rose. Also, a young unemployed couple from Cahors, and a middle-class girl who finds picking grapes more toilsome than she had expected. On the fourth day she puts down her basket and secateurs and leaves, not to be seen again. One young man is unemployed because he dropped out of school without the certificates you need if you are to push ahead. He has a flute which he sits outside with on still evenings, playing melancholy airs. His musical, sensitive soul does not come out in his table manners. He slouches head down into his food and gobbles with sounds like a delicate microphone picking up draining bathwater.

The journey to the vineyards is a sight characteristic of harvest time in the Lot, and, very likely, of wine areas round the world. The team stands in a bouncing cart towed by a

159

tractor driven by Monsieur Buzot. Attached to the cart is a mighty tub with a spiral of metal that mashes the grapes before they are tipped into the vats.

At the vineyard the workers collect secateurs and a basket. The secateurs are a problem as some are so blunt as to be useless, tearing the stalks instead of cutting them. Blunt secateurs slow you down, so when everyone else has reached the end of a row, whoever has blunt secateurs is still only halfway along. Habitués of the harvest naturally bring their own superior secateurs.

The pickers work in pairs, one on each side of the vine. They don't stay with the same partner, though by the third week Catherine and a young woman from Cahors tend to keep together, pleased in a women's-lib way at being able to advance more swiftly as a pair than the men. Catherine sometimes works, though prefers not to, with a little man named Quercy (of all things) who snips and picks at astonishing speed. He has a job with a taxi firm and comes to pick when he's not working his shift. He has twinkly brown eyes and looks like Mrs Tiggywinkle in the Beatrix Potter books. Working with Mrs Tiggywinkle is hazardous. You have to keep your fingers well clear of his darting secateurs or in a flash he will have them off and into the basket.

Snipping your fingers is always a risk. The vines are so leafy there is often no seeing the stalk, you have to grope for it. But if your hands are so cold you can't tell your fingers from the stalk, you can cut yourself. You can also snip a finger if your mind wanders, as it does, grape picking being extremely boring. When I show up one day to test the lunch I hear so much about, and to pay for it by picking, I almost lose a finger. No one warned me. The finger bleeds for half an hour. There is blood on my shirt and blood on the grapes. When this happens you bathe your finger in the pail of water kept for rinsing the secateurs, apply a plaster from the first-aid box beside the pail, and get back to work. Let's not talk about it.

The main problem is backache. The challenge is discovering the least uncomfortable position for hours of snipping. The lowest bunches of grapes hang close to the ground, and if you stoop, backache sets in quickly. On sunny days there is the added risk of sunburn in the gap where the shirt rides up from the top of the jeans. Kneeling works for a while but not where the ground is stony or waterlogged. Squatting is possible until pins and needles strikes. Sitting is useless, it is laborious, slow, and not to be attempted except in cases of extreme fatigue. Whatever varieties of position Catherine tries, at the end of each day she feels she has been moulded into a forward-bending U-turn. Monsieur Buzot suggests she sleep all night bent backward over a barrel. The first days are the most punishing. Later the body adapts. Staying stooped is fine. The ache comes when straightening up.

Still, grape picking must be preferable to picking pumpkins or water melons.

Cutting the grapes is a small art, as is positioning the basket so that the bunches will drop straight in. The Auxerrois grapes for Vin de Cahors are heavier and stickier than those for vin ordinaire. After finishing a row of Vin de Cahors the men's cigarettes stick to their fingers. Shaking hands is like dipping into glue. When a basket is full the picker carries it to the tub behind the cart or to big, washtub-shaped containers. The rim of the tub behind the cart is above head height so tipping the grapes in calls for muscle. Usually the men will empty the women's baskets. Catherine grants them that.

The harvesters talk as they work. 'Cat-air-een, écoutez!' Jean the Breton calls to Catherine from time to time, poking his head above the tops of the vines. 'My tailor is reech!'

At first she can't understand what he is trying to say. His conversation is generally bawdy and she sees nothing bawdy about Jean's tailor being rich, merely improbable. 'My tailor is rich' turns out to be the first sentence in a French-English phrase book of seventy or eighty years ago, perhaps the same phrase book Ginette brought for her crash course before she went off to London.

At quitting time the troops feel they have put in a solid day's work. They heave themselves into the cart, Jean takes up a privileged position behind Monsieur Buzot at the wheel of the tractor, and they rumble back to the farmhouse for a bath and repose until summoned to another grotesque dinner.

Grape picking has not made Catherine rich. Monsieur and Madame Buzot pay the minimum wage for France (Madame is the banker) and subtract board and lodging, though that is a paltry amount. For meals that would cost sixty francs in a restaurant the pickers pay around ten. They also have a choice between cash and the equivalent in wine. Catherine opts for some of each. She arrives back in the Place Clemenceau with puny wages but listing under the weight of gallons of red wine.

Speaking of weight, though I shouldn't, Catherine has gained twenty-two pounds. Three weeks to put on twenty-two unwanted pounds. Close on three months it will take for her to shed them and return to her sylph-like self. Polly finds Mrs Bunn in the Happy Families pack. She opens her mouth, catches my eye, and shuts up.

15 Exposing
the Beams

AFTER EIGHTEEN months renting on the Place Clemenceau we have bought a flat round the corner in the rue Nationale.

Monthly cheques to a landlord are francs down the plug. If we are to be in Cahors indefinitely, buying makes sense. The Crédit Agricole will surely lend us the money if I address them loudly enough in English, supported by Catherine making ingratiating noises in French. We have heard that banks are in a lending mood, also that the Crédit Agricole is the biggest bank in the world. The latter claim would seem unlikely were it not that France is top-heavy with farmers and agriculture: Europe's largest food producer and exporter, sixty per cent of the land farmland, with 265 varieties of cheese ('The French will only be united under the threat of danger. Nobody can simply bring together a country that has 265 kinds of cheese.' De Gaulle, 1951. With only slightly different wording, and a larger or lesser figure for the number of cheeses, also attributed to Churchill, Cocteau, and doubtless others). Perhaps the statistic I saw was that the Crédit Agricole is the biggest bank in the world for farmers. But it will accept money from anyone and presumably will lend too. The Cahors branch is currently bringing its charmingly mouldering premises on the Boulevard Gambetta into the 1980s with a façade of fine pre-stressed concrete and glass, and through its portals more glass, paintings by local artists, and lustrous floors. Not a place you would want farmers with dung on their boots traipsing in and out of, but clearly there is money to burn.

Catherine found the flat assisted by Gustave. I view it and shudder. It is a decayed warren, a labyrinth of absurd cubby holes. We would have six of these cells each, the girls included, with several over, and none sizeable enough to do more than yawn and stretch in. My head almost brushes the ceilings, especially where they sag, and I'm only five eleven and a half. Who lived here? Elves? At least the place has been stripped bare. The tidy elves took their toadstools and awls when they left, presumably for a place with fewer rooms. These rooms are good only as pantries for food. Perhaps that is what they were, the elves having been French and therefore food-minded. Catherine says the price is très intéressant, meaning not outrageous, perhaps even a bargain. She names the figure, astronomic and meaningless. I nod. (People say, 'Look up at the night sky! The Andromeda Galaxy alone contains two hundred billion stars and is two million light years away, can you imagine?' No, I can't. Figures over one hundred become progressively unreal.)

The situation in the heart of la vieille ville is a knock-out. The rue Nationale has massive carved fourteenth-century doors and windows and three baker's shops within twenty paces of each other. The approach from the street to the elves' flat is through dungeon doors, along a stone passage, and up a spiralling wooden firetrap of a stairway open to the blue empyrean. Above the stairway at roof level is a sheet of ill-fitted, flapping, corrugated plastic to hold off the worst of the rain. The flat occupies the entire fourth, topmost floor. Outside its crumbling brick walls is a sort of deeply fissured walkway or veranda which slants towards the stairwell and is supported by bent and rusted iron bars. At arm's length over the walkway's rail is a washing line where the elves used to hang out their smocks and leggings. Anyone hanging out the washing on the day the walkway gives way will be plunged down the stairwell to a splattery death but it will be quick. I tell Catherine the situation is stunning but actually to live here, wouldn't we have to take down perhaps two of the interior walls to create somewhere to sit and be together?

'Two walls?' cries Catherine. 'We gut it! The question is, are there *poutres?'*

Poutres – beams. Somewhere above the drooping ceilings is the roof. If, supporting the roof, are the original beams dating back to the fourteenth-century Capetians Louis the Quarrelsome and John the Posthumous, we will evidently abolish the ceilings, expose the beams, and glory in an effect *sensationel.*

A builder with ceiling-attacking tools is called in. The roof has beams, if not from the epoch of John the Posthumous, possibly from that of Charles the Mad (1380–1422). The Crédit Agricole lends us the money at eight per cent, which everybody says is très intéressant, we buy the flat, a ritual conducted with much signing in the presence of a lawyer and all manner of unidentified persons we never saw before and never will again, and are steered towards an architect.

Two architects, in fact. Monsieur and Madame Dessin, husband and wife. He takes care of the estimates and on-site capering, she the drawing-board and whatever is to follow the gutting. In practice their areas of responsibility overlap. When a knotty problem arises either can say that that is the area of expertise of the other, who happens to be away this week designing a château for the Duc de Dubois. From Monsieur I learn the terrifying word global as in prix global and somme globale, meaning lump sum, the grand total, the final reckoning, the last straw. Even at eight per cent I need to know this figure, not least because it keeps changing, especially in the design stage, but whenever Monsieur Dessin taps his calculator and announces with satisfaction the prix global, whatever it might be I have the feeling we are buying the planet. If an architect in England told his client, 'This is the global price', he would have no clients. We point out the slanting veranda supported by rods which buckle another millimetre downwards each time we look. How much to have the veranda fixed? Monsieur taps his calculator, frowns, and observes severely that the veranda is stronger than it looks, it has been there many years, but we shouldn't hold a party on it.

Catherine hits it off with Madame Dessin. They hold conferences at Madame's drawing board, imagination running riot and a flat being invented. I attend the early sessions but am dispensable. Catherine has the ideas and Madame the know-how. When I find reasons to be absent their protests are hollow. Each daughter will run away from home if she doesn't have her own room, so the flat will have four bedrooms, Lucy on the lower level and Kate and Polly in separate rooms under the roof, each with her own staircase. Two staircases won't be cheap but still, eight per cent. At a rare appearance at the drawing board I ask why Kate and Polly can't share a staircase, then, when they reach the top, shake hands and split to their separate rooms? I am gazed at with astonishment. The final plans provide for a single staircase. That is my contribution to our new flat.

Monsieur Dessin tells us that the builders will start work on Monday. Where and with what will they start and how long before we shall detect progress? On Tuesday, Catherine and I venture forth to take a peek, at lunchtime when the builders won't be there, if ever they arrived.

Where is the flat? Where the elves' warren, its doors and passageways? We blink at dust-filled emptiness confined by four walls. On the floor is a mountain of rubble. High above, beams hold up the tiled roof.

Months later the finished flat, so far as such an enterprise is ever finished, includes a spacious drawing-room or salon, whatever it is, with exposed and mighty beams. A masterpiece. The master's study is tiny but okay. No complaint at all. Snug is the word. I have a desk, chair, armchair, shelves, and three doors. One door leads to the master bedroom (bathroom en suite, quel luxe!), another to a passage to the hall, and the third to the slanting veranda outside, which one day we shall have to have attended to, preferably before it gives way. Fewer than three doors, I am instructed, would have meant completely altering the plans, possibly the abandonment of the entire project, and would have added a substantial sum to the prix global.

The happiest aspect of our very own flat is that through the dungeon doors below, turn left and walk three paces, stands the baker's with the best bread in Cahors.

Who says it is the best bread? We do. But this being France, where to dissent is a matter of self-respect, our friends debate the matter with passion.

A French person might privately agree but will publicly disagree simply to enliven the day. A cultural difference between the French and us Brits which takes a little getting used to is that French husbands and wives roundly disagree with each other in front of guests. Nobody is embarrassed apart from the English, and probably Americans, because that is how it is. Raymond and Ginette, Francine and Pierre, their voices rise, their cheeks redden, and spittle may bubble at the corners of their mouths as they contradict each other on the best route to Rocamadour, whether direct by Labastide-Murat or along the N20 then cut across. British spouses may disagree over whether the milk, if any, should go first into the teacup or into the tea after it is poured, but we do so in private. For quite a while I took it for granted that our French friends detested each other. They don't. They simply have no inhibitions about squabbling in front of an audience. Indeed they would be surprised to learn they were squabbling. They would call what they are doing the art of conversation. This art calls for interruptions which we would consider impertinent.

Conversation for the French is rapid, witty, give-and-take with constant interrupting, contradicting, endorsing, exaggerating, and digressing. Contrary to being impertinent, the French consider that conversation of this nature shows enthusiasm for the other's existence. What conversation is not, or shouldn't be, is delivering or listening to a monologue. Monologues are for the lecture hall and likely to be weary, stale, flat, and unprofitable. So we have only to mention the excellence of the bakery three paces from our dungeon doors and the table is in uproar. Everyone either has passionate praise for our baker or they would have him executed. They damn and exalt rival bakers and different breads.

'Baguettes – pfft!' exclaims Francine, smiting the table with her spoon. 'They are for making tyres!'

Pandemonium. All I said was that the baker below us on the rue Nationale makes bloody good bread.

A bread freak urges Catherine to try a boulangerie in a village forty miles away. The bakery there is so celebrated that people visit from far and near for its heavy, unrefined pain de campagne. Catherine, on a spare morning, drives off.

When she arrives at the shop the baker's wife refuses to sell her bread. She asserts that the bread is too good. Most of our bread goes to Paris, she announces. Is she now expected to sell to just anyone who happens to drop by? Catherine pleads that she hasn't just dropped by, she has driven forty miles expressly for Madame's bread. She virtually has to go down on her knees. The baker's wife steels herself to parting, grudgingly, sighing and muttering, with a loaf shaped like a swollen landmine and weighing about the same.

Fine bread it turns out to be, though I'd not make a habit of driving forty miles for it, and Catherine never goes again. After a week we have made only meagre inroads into our landmine loaf. We crumb some of it for treacle tarts and feed the rest to the swans in the park.

Polly has two best friends: gymnast Elsa, daughter of Françoise and Gimi, and Domie, whose parents live on the other side of the boulevard where the doctors and lawyers live in detached houses with rose gardens and a wall to keep the dogs in. Domie's parents' dog is a hyperactive spaniel named Coca-Cola. Her father has a new billiards table on which I am invited to play but the table turns out to have no pockets. What kind of billiards table has no pockets?

Either this is strange French billiards or he has been sold a dud. Domie's mother crosses the boulevard each day to buy her bread at Our Bakery.

Kate, old enough to ride her scooter, rides it to the stables, Polly as passenger, where they then ride Zazie, Duke, Hector, and the unendearing Bijou. Kate's best friend is Sylvie, another horseperson. When not at the stables or the cinema, Kate and Sylvie are to be seen puttering along the boulevard on a scooter, either Kate's or Sylvie's, to cafés where they join with friends to discuss the hit parade and foment revolution.

Lucy scintillates in a school production of a farce by Goldoni at the eighteenth-century Théâtre Municipale. (Ten years on, neither Lucy nor I can remember the name of the play. Goldoni, 'the Italian Molière', wrote over a hundred and fifty comedies, as many as Alan Ayckbourn.) Lucy is the chambermaid, not the leading role but a crucial one. She has to receive and deliver billets-doux and be duplicitous. Her mother and I sit in the dress circle biting our nails, waiting for her to forget her lines and drag the play to a stop. She does not forget them. I promise myself to be kind to Lucy from now on. At the interval we mill with doting parents whose offspring also have prominent roles. We chat with Pierre the Teacher who looks over our shoulders to see if there isn't someone more important he should be having a word with, exactly as during intervals in the West End.

Lucy's stage presence and talent for remembering her lines may have filtered down from my mother. I suspect that my mother might have liked to have gone on the stage professionally. She had a beautiful voice: low, lulling, expressive. As a young woman she acted with – the Huddersfield Thespians, was it? I have a photograph of her as Ophelia. For thirty years while we lived in Iver, near where my father built his matchless sewage plant, she played leading roles with the local drama society. She had me christened with the middle name Forbes because she was enamoured of the Forbes-Robertsons: Sir Johnston Forbes-Robertson (1853–1937), actor-manager ('. . . one of the finest voices ever heard on the stage . . .' *Oxford Companion to the Theatre*), his three younger brothers, all actors, and his daughter, Jean ('also an excellent actress'). She enjoyed charades and recitations. At the age of six I found myself on stage at a bleak hall in Slaithwaite (pronounced Slowit), a twopenny trolley ride from Huddersfield, facing an audience of ladies of the Women's Institute and reciting a comic north country poem of twenty or thirty verses which I knew by heart. Stanley Holloway ('Get me to the church on time') used to recite the same poem. The only lines I now remember are:

> 'Sam, Sam, pick oop tha musket,'
> The sergeant exclaimed with a roar.
> Sam said 'Tha knocked it doon Reet!
> Then tha'll pick it oop, or it stays where it is, on t' floor.'

Floor had two syllables – floo-ah. I forget the poet's name but he wrote one epic where Mr and Mrs Ramsbottom and their son Albert are on an outing to Blackpool zoo. Albert pokes his stick with an 'orse's 'ead 'andle into a lion's ear. The lion thereupon swallows Albert. Who can blame it? On stage at Slowit W.I., with scabbed knees and slipping socks, I went blank after two verses. Utter blankdom. Just the silent rows of expectant, encouraging W.I. faces, some beginning to giggle. Tears and rescue by Mummy.

Instead of going on the professional stage she worked for her newspaperman father, who founded the *Colne Valley Guardian*, a densely printed weekly, publication day Friday. He had a staff of five or six, at a guess, including his son and a grand-daughter. The companionable typesetter seated at his clanking, hissing machine, slotting in the type, would allow me to slot in selected little chunks of the silvery metal, a treat which palled after very few slottings. I would scurry along the ink-smelling corridor to the office where I could drool over shiny stills of the films playing that week in Huddersfield, and at Slowit's cinema, The Winston. James Cagney in *Angels with Dirty Faces. The Thief of Baghdad,* with Sabu. I cannot imagine that The Winston ever showed a French film.

My grandfather wrote the editorials, local politics, church notes, bowls club, Masonic Lodge, doings at Britannia Mill, Slowit's redbrick woollen textiles factory with a sky-high chimney, and book reviews. His bookshelves were filled with review copies of John Galsworthy, Hugh Walpole, and Edgar Wallace. My mother read proofs, trammed or trolleyed for advertisements to Linthwaite, Meltham, and Golcar, and wrote the births and deaths, Women's Institute, and forthcoming attractions.

With complimentary tickets she took me – and my brother if he was home from boarding school – to Huddersfield's exotic, gilded Theatre Royal. The shows were not always appropriate for a nine-year-old. *East Lynne,* if I remember rightly, had as its climax a bereft mother crying out like Medea over her dead child, 'Gone! And never called me mother!' A gross north-country comedian named Frank Randle headed a music-hall bill. He wore enormous boots and delighted the audience by continually belching. When he was not belching he was saying to his straight man, who would be standing on one of his big feet, 'Gerroff me foo-it'. He was enormously popular but rarely, if ever, invited onto BBC radio's variety shows.

Reporting an event in Huddersfield, once or twice at my tedious urging my mother would deposit me at a matinee at the Ritz and collect me when the programme was over. A soldier in khaki, ignoring a thousand empty rows where he might have spread out unhampered, sat beside me, covered our laps with his greatcoat, then unbuttoned and molested me. He must have been disappointed because there was very little to molest. When he tried to put my hand on his thing, I refused, and when he suggested we go to the gents – the sum total of our conversation – I shook my head. Small victories. The programme was half over before I found the sense and courage to change seats. He was a gormless soldier probably off to fight Hitler, perhaps to be killed. I did not tell my mother, waiting in the foyer, or anyone. Too shaming.

171

My brother inherited our mother's relish for amateur dramatics, though he might think relish is pitching it a little strong. He was Warwick in a school production of *Saint Joan*, and thereafter played numberless roles with various drama groups. In productions of *Toad of Toad Hall* he has by now played every part – Rat, Mole, Badger – except Toad and Second Rabbit. A solicitor recently retired to Devon, he joined the local drama society which promptly put on *Toad of Toad Hall*.

My mother approached her heavy part as the schoolteacher in *The Corn is Green* seriously enough to travel twenty miles to Reading for tips from a drama and elocution teacher, Maude Simpson, who had studied under Elsie Fogarty (as did Laurence Olivier), founder of the Central School of Speech and Drama. Mrs Simpson's name was tracked down by my Uncle Tom, my Dad's brother in Scotland. Uncle Tom was by training a pianist but he too had studied briefly under Elsie Fogarty. He believed that class (e.g. flawless diction) counts, and as I was at school in Reading suggested I should also go to Mrs Simpson, the sooner the better. Courtesy of Uncle Tom, I was given to understand that my accent was a mixture of Slowit and Slough and that I spoke with my mouth shut.

Mrs Simpson was a slender, articulate woman in a flowered dress. She had a fey daughter, Anne, aged thirteen. I was fifteen. More of Anne in a moment.

After our opening ten seconds of conversation Mrs Simpson began to eye me apprehensively. 'Have you lived in Australia?' she asked.

'Noaw,' I said.

She backed away. 'We need to do something about your vowel sounds,' she said.

Anne came feyly into the room wearing her school tunic, and I fell in love on the spot. Ignoring me, she told her mother she would be in the kitchen having cornflakes and departed in a mist of airs innocent, maiden manners, sweet looks, loose locks, long locks, lovelocks . . . Oh my!

Mrs Simpson spoke impeccably. 'This will not be easy,' she

said, meaning improving my speech, and opening her mouth so wide that an aeroplane could have flown in. She could have been captured the way explorers capture crocodiles by slipping a piece of wood vertically between its jaws. It was true, when I spoke I hardly opened my mouth at all. I opened it more to breathe than to speak. Mrs Simpson said that even my breathing was bad. (Breathing, not breath.) 'You will have to learn to breathe, Michael. Correct breathing is the basis of good speech.'

Having arranged me in an upright posture, head up, body balanced comfortably on the balls of the feet, arms akimbo, fingers curled, and knuckles resting lightly on either side of the ribcage, she took up a similar posture facing me. Together we started breathing. Not just any old breathing but deeply from the diaphragm. We breathed and counted. 'One two-o-o, one two-o-o.' It was exhausting.

Breathing is about all we did in the early lessons. The ribcage had to expand and contract in a fluid motion. Mrs Simpson would place her hands on the sides of my ribcage and command, 'Now! One two-o-o, one two-o-o.'

She explained that correct speech could be learned only after I had unlearned the bad habits picked up in Australia. We had to break before we could build. She produced anatomical charts showing the functions of the diaphragm, lungs, larynx, epiglottis, and uvula. She opened wide her mouth, mooed 'Oooh', and made me peer in at her jiggling uvula.

We tried vowel sounds. 'Ooh, aah, eeh,' I mouthed, sometimes singing the vowels to chords struck by Mrs Simpson on the piano. After five minutes of vowel sounds a drawn expression would creep over my speech doctor's face and she would sit down. Then she would resolutely rise. We would face each other again with our fingers on our ribcages and breathe. On occasion she would summon Anne into the room and make us work at breathing and vowel sounds together. Though Anne spoke as matchlessly as her mother she was too otherworldly to protest. 'Nobody can breathe too much,' Mrs Simpson would say.

173

With the passing of the months my passion for Anne held steady, though I never saw her except when she was called in and together we went 'Ooh, aah, eeh'. We progressed to poetry.

> She left the web, she left the lo-o-om,
> She made three paces through the ro-o-om.

One afternoon, Mrs Simpson out of the room on some household chore, I found myself alone with my love. 'Anne,' said I, 'let us not waste these moments. Let us do our breathing.' I assisted her into the correct posture, adjusting her knuckles on the sides of her ribcage. (O rare ribcage!) I stepped back six inches and took up a similar position. We faced each other with our hands on our ribcages, looked into each other's eyes, and breathed. Daringly I proposed, 'Shall we do our vowels?' Anne was not in love with me but she may have been very slightly in awe. I was older and bigger. 'Ooh, aah, eeh.' I was trying to catch a glimpse of Anne's uvula when Mrs Simpson came in. 'I see,' she said.

Instead of ordering me from the house she entered us, her daughter and me, for a poetry reading competition at her alma mater, the Central School of Speech and Drama. We would have to recite a Yeats poem, *I would that we were, my beloved, white birds on the foam of the sea,* and a poem of our own choice. Mrs Simpson chose for her daughter Gray's ode on the cat drowned in a goldfish bowl, and for me a Scottish ballad charged with ecstacy and bloody murder about Helen on Kirkconnell Lea. Helen is shot dead in verse two, whereupon the narrator and lover, me, draws his sword and slaughters the killer. 'I hackèd him in pieces sma'.' I was not to attempt a Scottish accent, Mrs Simpson instructed. I had not been going to. We practised our poems endlessly.

The competition at the Central School was ferocious. Hordes of trained offspring of actors and actresses bent on a career on the boards, next stop Hollywood, and judges who were former pupils of Elsie Fogarty, whom I was fed up hearing about. Neither of us won a major award but this time I did not forget my lines. We each came away with certificates of commendation. Anne's diction was as peerless as anyone's, judges included, but her presentation may have lacked fire. My performance was all fire, Slough, and Slowit. An old queen of a judge with wavy hair and probably make-up praised the power of my presentation but criticized my vowels as being too drawn out. I should learn not to linger over them, he said. I was tempted to tell him that was Mrs Simpson's doing. All those oohs, aahs, and eehs.

After a year the lessons stopped. Everyone had had enough. There is only so much an elocution teacher can teach. For the future it was up to me to practise daily in front of a mirror. You don't, though, do you?

The challenge of the poetry-reading competition did not bring Anne and me closer together. The truth is we were not suited. She was ethereal and I wanted flesh. I never got closer to her than helping her position her knuckles on the sides of her ribcage. I suppose that was better than nothing.

16 Academe, Sort of

I N ACADEME'S Cadurcien groves Catherine is busy with
ambitious private pupils. Their parents at any rate are
ambitious. She has one lad whose parents want him to enter
a military college, but for that he must score adequately in
English. If he fails to reach the necessary standard he will
become a policeman. The lad tells Catherine what he has
not told his parents, which is that he would prefer to be
a policeman. She is also teaching part-time at the École
Agricole. From the Crédit Agricole to the École Agricole.

She is not thrilled by her embryo farmers but she plugs
away, struggling to make the classes agreeable and useful
to hobbledehoys for whom English is neither, but who are
stuck with one hour a week of it. The only English they
will ever need they already have. Le disco, le hot dog, le
fast food, le sweat (sweat-shirt), le marketing, and cool,
as in C'est cool, though not as yet the full · C'est cool,
man. These are not lycée students who slog through three
hours of language classes a week, thirty-five weeks a year for
seven years – English is the first foreign language of choice
for nine out of ten students – and who are at least aware
that for a business career, showbiz, virtually any job with
a cosmopolitan touch, English will be handy because they
are likely to meet anglophones whose French will in most
cases be lousy. Even as lawyers, doctors, dentists, vets, with
no intention of venturing outside France unless on a cruise
ship to somewhere preferably French, like Guadeloupe, they

will have English-speaking customers with whom it will be impressive to be able to toss out phrases beyond 'My tailor is reech'. The myth in France is that after the long grind of English classes pupils emerge bilingual from the lycée. They seldom do, and those with fair English soon lose it from lack of use. I sympathize with them. Unless you happen to be a polyglot Anthony Burgess, foreign languages are a bugger.

So we should be kind to the French. They have surrendered the struggle to keep, as the common coin of international diplomacy and commerce, the language of Montesquieu ('Les Anglais sont occupés; ils n'ont pas le temps d'être polis.') and Montaigne ('Que sais-je?'). In 1992 the French government will introduce a curriculum change which will have children learning their first foreign language from the age of nine, not eleven as now. At eleven they will start a second language. The first optional foreign language being, for the overwhelming majority, English, the second is usually Spanish or German, in that order, Spanish being thought simpler to learn.

I digress like a French conversation. Catherine wants me to fill in for her one afternoon, teach English to her farmer boys and girls, because the class clashes with some more pressing matter and wouldn't it be a worthwhile, writerly experience for me? I say that as a writer I am able to imagine the experience in all its gruesomeness and would sooner not. She proposes I give them a history of jazz because the French are fanatical about jazz, I have all these jazz records, and if I keep playing Louis Armstrong and Bessie Smith I will hardly need to utter a word.

I construct a lecture on jazz with musical illustrations that would make an acceptable six-part series for BBC radio. The agape rustics in the classroom are more gripped by my French than by Louis Armstrong. It being clear from the empty stares which greet my slow and steady beginner's English that we are getting nowhere, I switch to a breezy, Alors, c'était les Nègres a Nouvelle Orléans après la guerre civile – Abraham Lincoln, okay? – qui a commencé, qui fait ou faisent commencer, zut, qui étaient responsables pour le commencement, le genesis, du jazz.' This is a strain for everyone. I kick off with King Oliver's *Dippermouth Blues*. They don't even tap their feet. They know only a French pop star improbably named Johnny Halliday, and France's top pop group of the eighties, Téléphone.

Catherine also ropes me in for one of her fortnightly conversation classes with two professional women who like to practise their not-bad English. The class is a five-minute walk away at the home of one of the women, lasts two to three hours, and is recompensed with a perfectly decent amount of francs. Soon I am giving this class regularly. Catherine is free to reclaim it but she is not eager. She says that after twenty minutes she runs out of topics to talk about. Who wouldn't? As it happens, I don't. At my first class – class is a bleak word for so civilized an evening – I accept the ladies' offer of a Scotch, rather to their surprise. The whisky is poured generously and neat. After it appears to have evaporated I protestingly accept a refill. They can't stop me talking. The bottle reappears at subsequent classes, and eventually a fresh bottle. The ladies drink herbal tea, sometimes a treacly liqueur, and practise their English when I shut up long enough to give them the chance.

Francine ropes me in to speak to her English class at Collège Gambetta, though only once. Meet the Author. The English textbook her class uses includes a spy story I wrote long ago for a children's anthology. This is the first I have heard of its transmogrification into a strip cartoon in the French school system. Royalties, if any, were unnoticeable. Never mind, soul is what matters, and the opportunity to stand up in front of a class of thirteen-year-olds, tomorrow's leaders of France. Francine does not mind what I talk about as long as I speak my normal English (refined Slowit and Slough, little does she know). Her class's English is good, she says. She herself speaks to them in brisk, fluent English. The class has the fevered, hopeful look of Old Testament people being told by Jeremiah that they must reform or else. When I speak slowly and simply Francine says I mustn't speak like that, I must speak normally, the class will understand. They don't give me the impression that they will. They are not springing from their seats to show off their English. Perhaps the presence of an authentic rosbif, creator of their textbook's strip cartoon, inhibits them. When one of the class, egged on by Francine, stiffens the sinews sufficiently to put up her hand and dare English, I have difficulty understanding her, thereby embarrassing everyone. Far more embarrassing than failing to be understood in a foreign language is failing to understand your own language spoken by those who think they have got it right. To cheer us all up I switch to my creative French, lots of exclamatory 'Dis-donc!', 'Tiens!', 'Alors!', 'Allez!', even 'O la la!' – all in everyday use, all meaningless. Francine is disapproving. Afterward she says the class was a great success.

Francine and a hairy, intense young man, and perhaps others, plan to found the Ciné-Club de Cahors. She summons Catherine and me to a meeting of film intellectuals at which aims and costs are thrashed out. The films will not be the usual *Battleship Potemkin* and *Cabinet of Dr Caligari*, which as highbrows we have all seen more than once, but recent foreign films of stature which never arrive in Cahors. The Ciné-Club gets off the ground and even thrives. Some of the films enrich our lives, others the reverse, such as the three-hour saga of contemporary Russian life which empties the cinema of all but the most masochistic faithful. Either Francine or the articulate young man mounts the stage to introduce each movie. The young man is strong on camera angles and editing. Francine asks us to watch out for the female psychology, advising us where we will find especially significant examples.

These films with female psychology always have a heroine, a morose woman of striking blonde beauty, staring without expression at the kitchen wall and suffering, but keeping going while her husband or lover is away fighting a war, or demonstrating for freedom against brutal riot police, or proving a point about his soul by climbing a mountain which could kill him. Often the husband doesn't come back, either because he is dead or he can't face being with the woman moving sensitively from room to room, touching a chairback here, stopping to look at a wall there. She does all this in silence, not so much as a flute for background music. I wouldn't have gone back either, even if she is as gorgeous as Ingrid Bergman. We see quite a few of these lugubrious films, stiff with female psychology, and made by directors named Wim Wenders, Herzog, Fassbinder, and, I suppose, the other Bergman.

In July and August the Ciné-Club goes into suspension along with everything else except visitors. High summer tends to be visiting time in Cahors.

In the years we have now lived here we have played host and hostess to motley youth, many of whom we have never seen before and never will again. It is inevitable and generally all right. If they were older they might bring news of Britannia more penetrating than 'Just the same' and 'Raining when we left', but then again they might not. A quartet of deferential students from London, roughing it round the Continent, and led by a daughter of friends, pitch their sleeping bags in the salon. Thirty similarly polite students from the Long Island college where I taught arrive bearing their bread, cheese, fruit, and cans of Coca-Cola, and picnic under the exposed beams. Then they move on to hotels. For ten days we have two pale, quiet lassies from the Cahors-Dumfries exchange, bewildered by all things French. A silent lad from Wigan, tough as nails, stays overnight and wordlessly eats copious shepherd's pie. We walk to the floodlit stadium to watch him dash and tackle. He is one of a junior rugby team from Lancashire playing against the Cahors junior team. France's south-west is rugby country: Beziers, Narbonne, Agen, Auch, Angoulême, Montpellier, Tarbes, Toulouse, Perpignan, Carcassonne.

Our offerings of hospitality are small beer compared with those of Elizabeth and Jean, succourers of strays, including their excessively friendly dog, Fanny, a mix of Gordon Setter and Cocker Spaniel, they think. The Honours List has announced that Elizabeth is to be awarded the MBE for services to Anglo-French amitié in the Lot. She journeys to Buckingham Palace with Jean, whose headgear is received by a liveried footman and hung on a peg – sole beret in a row of toppers.

Beautiful guardsmen stood on the stairway, Elizabeth narrates on her return. The room was magnificent. Huge chandeliers. Everything was huge. In the gallery a band of more guardsmen played popular, forgettable tunes (she has forgotten what). Outside the spring day was cool but no rain. Elizabeth (our Cahors Elizabeth) wore a blue coat and skirt with cream hat and shoes. The Queen wore a plain blue dress with a string of pearls and a diamond brooch. The Queen said, 'I'm very pleased to give you this decoration. What did you do for it?' Elizabeth said she was President of the Association France-Grande Bretagne in Cahors. The Queen said, 'Oh, you live in France, do you?' She extended her hand and that, Elizabeth tells us, was that. Not a scrap of food nor drop of drink. That side of the event, Elizabeth has not the least doubt, would have been better ordered in France.

After the visitors, Catherine and the girls board Scotland-bound coaches with Elizabeth and Jean, Gustave, Scotland-struck Françoise, and tribes of unruly Cadurcien whelps who are not going to be happy with the food that lies ahead: cock-a-leekie, clapshot, bawd bree, rumbledethumps, kippers, porridge. The next summer Catherine goes with a similar crew to Yugoslavia. Elizabeth, Jean, and Françoise bow out, this being a schools trip, not the Association France-Grande Bretagne.

I have a haircut before, light of heart, swanning off to anglophone London. I have failed to find in Cahors an inexpensive barber's such as the one at Fulham Broadway where the electric shears go zzzzz as in the army and the result is horrible but quick and cheap. A haircut's a haircut. You can get an expensive haircut that is horrible, it just takes longer. Cahors has no barber's shops that I have been able to discover, only unisex hair-styling salons. You have to have an appointment. The staff are begowned, perfumed demoiselles and there are plenty of them, one for the obligatory shampoo (quite enjoyable), another for the actual scissoring and the stepping back to survey progress, probably someone else to file your nails, though I have escaped that so far, and a trainee who brings coffee. On this occasion the nubile Mademoiselle who is to perform the scissoring seats me and asks if Monsieur would care for a magazine. Why not, thank you, say I. These sessions take time and she is evidently no keener to make conversation than I am. She trips away, returns, and places *Playboy* in my lap.

Any anthropologist worth his salt would know what this says about French cultural characteristics – matter-of-factness in matters of sex? concern that the male libido be catered to at all times? female flirtatiousness? – but I remain at a loss. Possibly she meant to bring *Motoring Magazine* and scooped up *Playboy* in error. Perhaps she is unfamiliar with the contents of *Playboy*, or sufficiently familiar to know it might have articles and fiction worth attention. Does she hand *Playboy* automatically to her Frenchmen customers and do they actually open it? If I open it it will open not at the printed word but inevitably at a full-frontal. There will stand my hair stylist with her scissors and comb looking down at the top of my head while her client looks down at art studies. Perhaps it is a test, but of what? I hand back *Playboy* with an apology but I have changed my mind, I shall meditate. Have I passed the test or failed?

Away to London then, freshly coiffed. In London I shall reacquaint myself with the real world, not least pork pies. Not flashy Harrods pork pies either but the little Lyons and Bowyers ones that once cost 18p, stealthily rose to 27p, and now are 34p. They are still wondrously gristly and still I can't say if I like best the gristly meat with its white globs of fat, the outer crust, the soggy inner crust, the wobbly ridge of jelly, or the air pockets brought on by age and shrinkage. What I can say is that there is nothing like them in Cahors.

Another autumn, another rentrée, and Kate's rentrée is to a hotel school in Toulouse. Reputedly this is one of the top two or three hotel schools in France and attached to a hotel, run by the students, which has a 'very comfortable' recommendation in the red *Michelin*. All the same, hardly the sort of Academe I had anticipated for her. Why does she not carry on to her baccalauréat in Cahors, next on to Oxford, Harvard, the Sorbonne, one of those, then a dazzling career as a High Court judge or editor of *The Times*? She prefers to go to hotel school, c'est tout. Never assume.

Off she goes, Kate the Waif, not yet sixteen, carrying her new knife box containing a carving knife, knife for gutting fish, other speciality knives, a corkscrew, spatulas, and suchlike professional equipment. In her suitcase, her waitress's outfit with a white apron to go over the black skirt, a pen for taking orders, and two linen napkins to drape over her arm while serving. For kitchen work she has two blue aprons for washing up, six cloths for drying dishes, basic jeans for absorbing spurting, boiling fat, and sneakers for splashing through pools of grease.

Kate's shell-shocked Dad (her Mum takes all this in her stride) none the less hoped she would do well at the interview and told her that she would be asked why she wanted a hotel career, to which she should respond that hotels had always fascinated her, they were a self-contained world, from the chambermaids and washers-up up to head chef and chairman of the board. The interview lasted five minutes – two men and a woman, all very friendly. When they asked why she wanted a hotel career, Kate said that hotels had always fascinated her, they were a self-contained world, from the chambermaids and washers-up up to head chef and chairman of the board. For the interview she scored nineteen out of twenty, higher marks than she had ever received for anything. Being bilingual probably helped.

On her first day, Kate tells us, she and her class are addressed by Monsieur le Directeur. He is youngish, in his thirties, bespectacled. He tells the class to work hard, to be smart, not to wear jeans except in the kitchen, not to leave the school in school hours, and that everyone would improve their job prospects by staying four years, better still six, rather than two. Kate never sees Monsieur le Directeur again.

Every weekend she comes home to Cahors. On her first weekend home she practises carrying six plates at once, five along the arm and the sixth in the hand for scraping leftovers onto. Catherine and I cannot watch. We leave the flat. She has learned to chop vegetables fast without chopping her fingers off, we all hope. In her third week she and her class cook their first meal and other students eat it in the canteen. Trout. Another class gutted the trout. The trout-gutting class. Kate's class roll the trout in flour and fry them in oil, making sure the head is to the left of the pan, the stomach facing forward. When her class learns to gut trout, one icy fish after another, the teeth scratch her fingers and her hands develop frostbite.

Some waif, Kate. She ends up staying the maximum six years at hotel school, a fairly rare phenomenon, the majority of students leaving after two, unable to wait before finding a hotel or restaurant where they can earn money. Four years bring her the equivalent of the baccalauréat because the training is not all trout and carrying six plates at once. There is maths, French, another language, usually English, history, geography, drawing, law, accountancy, commerce, typing, hotel management, and oenology. The oenology teacher is evidently elderly, cuddly, and keeps falling asleep in class. After four years of the chemistry of fermentation, crates of wine arrive in the classroom, and soup bowls into which to spit. The bowls go back to the kitchen as clean as they came out of it, and the wine bottles return empty. Boys take a course in electricity, girls in linen, meaning ironing. One of Kate's teachers of English discusses a text and admits he is not sure what Hershey means but believes it is a medal. Kate volunteers that it is a brand of American chocolate. The teacher puts her at the back of the class and ignores her from then on.

Most of her cookery teachers are young and have a substantial belly from the relentless tasting. Kate's favourite is the cakes and pastries teacher, not least because pâtisserie classes are calmer than the heat and bedlam of trout, soup, noodles, potatoes, all that, and she enjoys the swooning smells of apple tarts, profiteroles, crème caramel, and cheese soufflé. The pastry teacher is allergic to flour. If he touches flour he comes out in a rash. A student mixes the flour and fat and when the dough is ready the teacher takes over.

Unlike some of the training she is stuck with – making beds, scrubbing floors, and *plonge*, which is washing dishes – Kate finds her teachers likeable, though obsessed with cleanliness. You might ruin a meal with terrible cooking but you will receive a decent mark if you clean up and leave everything spotless after you have ruined it. The teachers never become cross when, for example, panicky students waiting on table in the restaurant gallop about bumping into each other, dropping plates and glasses, and one of them (not Kate) spills a sauceboat of parsley and garlic sauce over a customer. The teachers' attitude is that accidents happen so get them behind you now, while serving students, rather than when you are qualified and expert, or supposed to be, and bringing the parsley and garlic sauce to a grand lady with orchids in her décolletage. They get cross if the sauce goes over and someone laughs. Chances are that he who laughs will be made to clear up the mess.

The students eventually specialize in either *cuisine*, the kitchen, or *salle*, which is all the rest – waiting, housekeeping, reception, management. Kate opts for *salle*. I am mightily relieved. She arrives home one weekend with statistics showing that of all trades and professions that of chef has the highest murder rate. This is because of the stress, the heat, and having knives and gallons of booze to hand. Kate's statistics do not reveal whom chefs murder. Other chefs, presumably. The waiters and waitresses. There must be times they would be happy to murder the customer.

Kate's disaster happens not at the school but in the field, so to speak, whither students are despatched in the summer. In the perspective of eternity the calamity is not so terrible. Nobody is murdered. But while serving at a seafood restaurant at Port Grisson, on the Mediterranean, she is told to carry into the restaurant a king platter of seafood. 'Spectacular stuff,' Kate tells us later. 'Crab, oysters and mussels on an elevated dish above a main platter of sea snails and ice. Ice everywhere. It weighed a ton. It was bigger than me. I told them, "I'm not going to be able to do this." They said, "Yes you are", and pushed me through the swing door into the dining-room. The whole thing began to slide. I couldn't hold it. The lot went onto the floor.'

Kate tells us she has two particularly vivid memories of hotel school: the grind of sweeping and scrubbing kitchen and restaurant floors, and stunning exchanges with catering schools abroad.

In three weeks in Heidelberg her class drinks kegs and kegs of beer and oceans of wine. At a wine tasting they receive a dozen German white wines for every four students and nothing to eat except little bits of cheese. They guzzle and learn Bavarian drinking songs. In Glasgow the ambiance is whisky and bagpipes. The French students fall in love with Scotland. When not testing the single malt or shouting to be heard above the bagpipes they are singing *Auld Lang Syne*. They are taken on an outing to a loch but cannot see it because of fog. At least fog is the reason Kate gives for nobody seeing the loch.

School days, school days! Happy golden rule days!

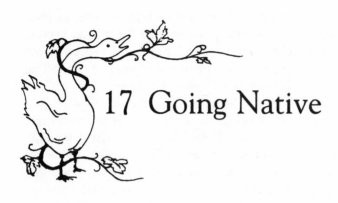

17 Going Native

T HE BRITISH who have transplanted to the Lot are a mix. The long and the short and the tall. Some have ample money, others hardly a penny. Some wear Harris tweed, others dress Frenchly in raiment from the local couturiers, whoever they may be, or from a stall in the market. We are not a clique, banding together for bridge and sundowners, swapping *The Times* for the *Telegraph* after we are done with the crossword, and excluding the French. The natives are friendly and I notice no cold-shouldering of them. On the contrary, we court them, some of them. Were we to reject them – an absurd proposition, what would be the point of being here? – they rightly wouldn't care, being French. 'Bof!' they would dismissively utter, hunching their shoulders, spreading their palms, and emitting either the blubbery little French raspberry, or, if out of sorts, 'Dis-donc!' and 'Alors!' with retching sounds like Maurice Chevalier singing *Louise*. We have no British Club, Anglophone Alliance, or Society of the Sons and Daughters of John Bull. We have the Association France-Grande Bretagne, aiming to draw the two nationalities together and of modest membership. We are a harmless, minuscule minority, not taking jobs away from the locals and not smashing the place up hooligan-style.

I like to think we are not merely tolerated but quite enjoyed, if only as the butt of good-natured, repetitive jokes about the Hundred Years War, our soggy climate, inedible food, and sexual mores (cold, inhibited, and homosexual, due to the dreadful weather, food, and such monasteries as Eton where we all go to school). The entente is cordiale. Having lived with or adjacent to Albion's perfidy for centuries, our hosts easily shrug off such exquisite arrogance as our calling the English Channel the English Channel when it's not English at all, it's La Manche, The Sleeve, n'est-ce pas? We Brits are a few floating, disparate ingredients, adequately nourishing and digestible, in the clear broth that is the Lot.

What the Lotois have no reason for knowing is that we have little in common with each other beyond possessing British passports (Irish in Catherine's case) and speaking French not always as she should be spoke, though on good days we try hard to improve. What we do share, individually or as couples, is a certainty that we are more intimate with and better understand our French neighbours than all the other British do theirs.

(Not, naturally, the few with a French spouse, such as Elizabeth, who are daily and visibly close to the French, or at any rate to the spouse. Probably not Jeffrey and Sally either, too involved with their painting to be concerned whether or not they may be inching towards tutoyer terms with the cheesemonger.)

The British here vie with one another in being best friends with the natives. They would deny it, perhaps not even comprehend that this is how it is, and as vanities go it is an innocuous one. But if John and Mary feed Farmer Leblanc's dogs all weekend while he and Madame have to be off to Brive, and farmer Leblanc then presents them with two gallons of wine, John and Mary will casually let us know about it as evidence of their total integration in la vie Lotoise. Jim and Peggy Wolfe are not alone in giving Christmas presents to their country neighbours. They receive in return jars of goose confit and bottles of quince liqueur, and tell amusing anecdotes about Dédé and Desirée and old Anatole, with whom they are on first-name terms. They give a Harrods blanket to a farmer with a game leg.

If I have neglected to mention Lana and Dick in this chronicle it is because they live fifty kilometres away so we don't see much of them. They have gone native, Lana especially. Should we worry about them? Dick was a museum curator in London. Lana, a former actress, is an impressive cook and getting better all the time, as are many of the Brits here: imaginative, experimental, given to adventure, which the French are not. Invited to eat at a French home, Catherine and I play the game, Guess what we will be having for dinner, and nine times out of ten we're spot on. What we and our compatriots do not do, but Lana does, is put on a Lucullan banquet for the neighbourhood peasants three times a year. One by one she will surely kill them off with culinary thrombosis. The peasants bring gifts of walnuts, ducks, geese, and the products thereof. Lana makes pastis: not the aniseed liquor but the pastry speciality which takes months to make, needs a half mile of table for rolling out each leaf of pastry, and cannot be made by anyone who has not lived in the Lot for fewer than fourteen generations, or not until Lana came along. She force-feeds her own geese and ducks for foie gras. 'They don't suffer,' she says. 'Do you see them running away from me?' She probably does the slaughtering. I am not about to ask. Tiresomely, like so many cooks who put on a sumptuous feast, she does not eat much herself.

For going native, becoming more Lotois than the bemused Lotois, brownie points are to be won. It's all related to food. What else would the immigrants and the natives have in common? The immigrants are for the most part former urban professionals with university degrees. The Lotois I am talking about here are farmers. Assemble a couple of Brit couples at a café on the Boulevard Gambetta on market day and they will rival each other with examples of their intimacy with the farmers. In England the equivalent farmer probably would not be given the time of day. ('Your true Cornish pasty, sor, 'as only spuds and onions.' 'Really, my good man.') (Then again, perhaps he might. 'Wrong, Farmer Giles! The Cornish pasty must have mutton!') But do we detect a jot of condescension, a tittle of complacency, among the expats? A belief that we are doing the peasants a favour by being friendly? An endorsement now and for ever of the Flanders and Swann ditty, 'The English, the English, the English are best, I wouldn't give tuppence for all of the rest!'?

Yes.

The condescension and complacency are so mild as to be unobjectionable. I find it so anyway. The wheels of neighbourliness are oiled by the giving and receiving of goods and services and by time-passing chat. Expats have the satisfaction that they are truly in France. The peasants neither tug their forelock nor torch the expats' houses. Everybody wins. To knock the element of condescension would be too solemn.

It is not just the Brits either. We meet a couple of retired Americans from the West Coast who have bought a summer home an hour's drive away, halfway to Bordeaux. When they are not telling us of the work they are having done on their house (I close my ears to details of cesspools and roofbeams) they are enthusing about their farmer neighbour, a gem, whom they know so well, he has these amusing ways, and so forth.

Catherine and I are not immune. We succumb to the we-must-be-close-to-the-natives urge. Naturally, not too close, not more than one encounter per week, with which the natives would heartily agree. What do I care about crop rotation, or Farmer Leblanc about the Yorkshire cricket score? But in our Catus days we brought whisky to the Becquets, and on our daily drive with the girls to the village school we gathered up fellow-scholar Patrick, scrubbed and uncertainly smiling, waiting for us among the leaves and chickens. Came the end of term, Monsieur and Madame Becquet gave us chickens stuffed with truffles and invited us into their kitchen for wine, marc, and biscuits from the village grocery.

If somewhere a reader is rolling his eyes skyward and throwing up aghast arms at my condescending use of the word peasant, too bad. Les paysans – peasants – is what the country people of the Lot are. Teachers and shopkeepers in Cahors speak without condescension of les paysans. Les paysans are those who bring to market melons, cèpes, rabbits, and dirt-besmirched eggs, free-range and fresh (except when eight out of ten are sulphurously rotten, as was the case with one batch we bought). Paysan is a derogatory term only in the mouths of vacationing Parisians who employ it indiscriminately for all inhabitants of the Lot and la France profonde generally, doctors and lawyers included.

What do they think of us, these Lot peasants with whom we interloping Brits vie for intimacy? If they think of us at all, I hope they do so uproariously at their kitchen table, enjoying themselves at our expense. I like to imagine them guffawing, banging the table with their spoons, and quaffing another bumper of rouge as they regale each other with their latest experience of the most odd and comical anglais.

Going on seven years since we came to Cahors, the past three in our own and the Crédit Agricole's home with the beams above, and below the most satisfactory bakery on earth. Polly has her own second-hand scooter. If she is a little under the legal age she is still a born scooterer and her scooter endows her with invaluable, life-enhancing independence. Simplifies her parents' lives too.

The parents, returning from an exhilarating evening at the Ciné-Club in which a Nordic beauty spends two hours feeling suicidal but doing nothing about it, discover Polly standing at the corner of the Place Clemenceau with said scooter and her pal, Elsa. Standing over them are two uniformed flics, cops. Omigod. What now have these children suffered, perpetrated? They have, says the more vocal flic, ridden this machine up and down the boulevard illegally, the machine not being equipped with obligatory passenger seat if two are to ride together, plus other machine-related irregularities, such as faulty lights, brakes, and where are their helmets? Be stopped for an offence by the police and other offences invariably pile up. We await the question: How old is Mademoiselle? They don't ask. Will a hundred-franc note get us off the hook? Too risky. Expensive too.

My tactic is to agree wholeheartedly with the Law, shaking my head at the barefaced cheek of youth, and sighing in gratitude at the alertness of the police. Catherine pleads in crafty subjunctives. The flics advise us to keep a tighter rein on these mademoiselles before they become incurably delinquent, and to be sure that the machine is attended to.

The older that children become, the more mobile. This means that Mum and Dad no longer have to ferry them everywhere. That means we shall never ever impound their machines, either as punishment or because they are trivially faulty. The machines can be fixed by the mechanically-minded among their stream of boyfriends. At eventide and on weekends, arsenals of post-pubertal male accoutrements bestrew the hall carpet and pile up in corners. Black leather jackets, motorbike helmets, greasy gloves, a finished bottle of Evian, an occasional kitbag of deferred homework. From above hammers rock music. Cigarette smoke seeps down the single stairway. I retreat to my study with its three doors. I disapprove mightily of these whiskery hunks and spotty nerds named Yves and Gilles and Etienne, not that I ever glimpse them, undiscovered as I am behind three shut doors. None are good enough for my daughters. Apart from anything else they are foreigners. In fact one is a very decent bloke, Michel, on course to become a quantity surveyor, which sounds like a proper job. He is still a foreigner. He is also too old for Kate – eighteen – and in any case due to be marched off for his year's military service. Even before he is marched off, un deux, un deux, Kate gives him the heave-ho. 'We're going to stay good friends,' she tells us. The only British boy we know is Sebastian, son of Jeffrey and Sally, but he is not yet ten and preoccupied with chess.

Polly receives a bee outfit for her birthday for wearing to parties. She dresses in furry black and yellow stripes and antennae and buzzes on her scooter along the boulevard going 'bzz bzz' at pedestrians. Returning one dark night on foot from the cinema, she and Elsa are flashed. The flasher inquires, 'Elle est belle, oui?' Polly, howlingly chanting 'Elle est belle, elle est belle, elle est belle, belle, belle!', sprints with Elsa from the flasher, Elsa losing a hairgrip in the grand dash. Polly will insist she agreed simply, 'Elle est très belle,' then ran, but family myth clings to the chanted, more rhythmic version. Why the flashed item should be the feminine belle, not a masculine beau, I have no idea and don't ask. Some reference in Lot patois, perhaps.

Poor Poll. She awakes one morning to the tintinnabulating of the alarm clock she herself set. She staggers from the flat with her school satchel, along the rue Nationale, through the Place Clemenceau, onto the Boulevard Gambetta. Dark, deserted Cahors. Unemptied garbage pails. Polly's watch registers an unholy wee hour but her watch has erred before. Is it Bastille Day? Christmas? The clock on the Mairie, never mistaken, says 5 a.m. Polly returns to bed for three more hours' sleep.

One Sunday she returns with Kate from the stables where they have ridden in an examination – judges and certificates – they have practised for and worried about for weeks. Kate has passed, Polly has failed. For ten minutes they say not too much, then Polly breaks down in tears. It's only horses, I tell her; she rides superbly, like John Wayne, the examiners are dolts and anglophobes. (The anglophobes passed Kate but this is no time to split hairs.) Kate too consoles. 'I'm the only one in the junior group who passed,' she again tells Polly. 'It's because Bijou reared and I hung on, I didn't fall off. If I hadn't hung on I'd have been thrown and killed. You'd have hung on. You ride as well as me. Better.'

Polly sobs, inconsolable. How cruel, grown-ups. Enough to turn one into a lifelong misanthrope.

Jim and Peggy Wolfe are talking about emigrating to Tasmania where Peggy has children and Jim step-children, step-grandchildren.

*

193

Monsieur Foissac, our sceptical schoolmaster friend in Catus, a lovely fellow, correct every time he happily grumbles, 'C'est le commerce,' has died of lung cancer. He was barely fifty.

Lucy passes her bac'. Do values exist? Ask the philosopher. She has decided to spend the coming months, (a) au-pairing in the United States, (b) cramming for one of the pickier British universities. She will need to shine in the entrance exam because the university may be unimpressed by her schooling in various countries and, who knows, positively prejudiced against France. ('Where did you say Cahors is?')

Au-pair to be, she flies to Seattle where she is immediately put under arrest. The first we learn of it is a postcard saying she is under guard in a motel at Seattle Airport, awaiting trial, but she loves us. The guard (female and two or three years older than Lucy) has the bed nearest the door in case Lucy attempts to escape.

I blame myself. I should have been savvy enough to impress on Lucy that you don't arrive in the US on a tourist visa and tell Immigration you have work as an au-pair. The US is waist-deep in illegal Irish au-pairs but the Irish know the ropes. They have associations with classes and lawyers instructing them exactly how to enter the US and how to survive illegally once in. Lucy's alternative to taking the next flight back whence she came, which she can't because she doesn't have the fare – she has about fifty francs – is to go before the judge. As it is a long holiday weekend there is no judge, so she remains incarcerated with her guard in the motel room, watching TV and eating bring-in pizza. When the judge shows up for work, the master of Lucy's au-pair family is at her side, swearing that though she is to stay with his family she will not be working, Your Honour, and won't be paid. The judge releases Lucy to the master, who happens to be a lawyer. Being a lawyer he can hardly go back on his word to the judge, probably a golfing partner. Unpaid Lucy changes the baby, feeds and reads to the four-year-old, and after a few weeks moves on to parents who shunt a little pocket money her way.

Equipped with a resident's permit, and paying income tax to the Fifth Republic (President Giscard d'Estaing now out, President Mitterand in), we are permitted a job if we want one and can find it. Catherine enters the employ of the tourist office as a guide, showing tour groups the Pont Valentré and leading them through alleys to brickwork of mind-bending historicity. Is she robbing a local of a job? I doubt it. She swots hard, poring over street maps, ingesting medievalism. I tell her to invent, the tourists are not going to know. This is not invariably the case. One or two challenge her on the authenticity of a door, or want to know the staple diet of the Quercynois in the fourteenth century. Françoise tells her these troublemakers are Parisians. She may be right. The French tourists who are not Parisians, and all the Dutch, Germans, Scandinavians, and British, are lambs.

Catherine also launches into a bachelor's degree in English at Toulouse University. She has diplomas in social science from Trinity College, Dublin, and in education from London, but further qualifications would be no handicap if she is to advance in teaching English as a foreign language. Term time, once a week, she boards the slow train to Toulouse. Her professors vary from the stony woman of the When-I-want-imagination-I-shall-ask-for-it school to the laid-back, left-wing, long-haired, corduroyed young structuralist who turns his chair round and sits with his arms wrapped round its back. We read – Catherine presents me hopefully with texts to analyse and assess – Shakespeare, Hardy, Hemingway, short stories by an Australian whose name I forget, and *Martin Eden*, by Jack London, which has surely dropped into the syllabus in error. Does Jack London have the same cachet with the French as Jerry Lewis and Woody Allen? I am excused the structuralism. Catherine writes her thesis on 'The Traditional and Modern Role of Woman in Thomas

Hardy's *Tess of the D'Urbervilles* and *Jude the Obscure*', quoting generously from the sixties gurus, Betty Friedan, Kate Millett, and Germaine Greer. I am not around when she receives her degree.

Whether in the traditional or modern role, Catherine has been 'seeing' Gustave.

Cuckolded by a Frenchie! Zut! The very stuff of farce!

I am probably the last to know. Even our dashing dentist, Jean-Philippe, father of two, has tried to tell me, but what we don't care to know we don't hear. I hear only 'Craches!' I am a prisoner in the padded chair. Again, 'Craches!' Jean-Philippe emotionally cries. It sounds like 'Crash!' which makes no sense. He is jabbing a finger in the direction of the porcelain bowl with the piddling fountain. Of course, *craches!* – spit! He demands to know why I put up with it and wants me to kill Gustave.

We soldier on, Catherine et moi, but Gustave and his poorly back don't seem to go away. Instead of killing him I accept an invitation to a repeat teaching performance on Long Island. This time I go alone. Perhaps one academic year and distance will sort things out.

Adieu, Cahors. Scrubby hills of the Lot, bye-bye. Not that I am aware the farewell is to be permanent. Sylvette trips up to the apartment with a parting gift of truffled goose pâté.

I sail from Le Havre on a French cargo boat, the *Atlantic Cognac*, which sounds promising. She has a sister cargo boat, the *Atlantic Champagne*, which would have done equally nicely. Cargo boat is pricier than jetplane – involving after all a private cabin and ten days of French cuisine – but a magazine is paying and will receive a cargo-boat article.

Mid-Atlantic. All seems calm enough but a storm is blowing up. My writer's observational powers forewarn me that something might be afoot when matelots bustle about anchoring tables and chairs and telling us passengers to clear our shelves of all things loose and movable. The boat pitches and rolls. At the top of a companionway I bump into the skipper, a salt from Nantes. 'Bonne chance, mon commandant!' I tell him. 'Pourquoi, bonne chance?' says he, shirty, as if by wishing him good luck I cast doubt on his competence.

Next day, the sea settled to mere choppiness, we share a bottle of champagne. He says these crossings can be lonely, ten days with only his small crew, whom he knows too well, and four passengers. More than four passengers and the ship must take on a doctor. Two days from New York he halts the *Atlantic Cognac*. At our rate of knots we will arrive too soon, which evidently we must not do. The sun shines and for an afternoon we idly float. Alone, alone, all, all, alone; alone on a wide, wide sea. The chef arrives on deck with a bowl of shrimp for bait. The crew line the side of the boat casting fishing lines into the glassy wilderness of ocean. The catch is thirty kilos of mackerel, hake, haddock, and pollack, for supper.

At Port Elizabeth, New Jersey, two customs officers board. Sylvette's jar excites their curiosity. I had supposed it might. Unrefrigerated truffled goose pâté, speckledy-grey and lumpy, shifts and squirms as the customs officers hold the jar to the light, turn it upside down, shake it, and pass it in puzzlement one to the other. It's touch and go whether they will permit this glory of the Lot into hygienic America, to date free of dreaded truffled goose pâté disease. Will they remove it with tongs to a bath of acid? They hand it back, convinced, I imagine, that no one in his right mind will ever open it.

Apart from one week the following year when we sell the London house and shift its shiftables to the rue Nationale, and I stuff myself with bread from the bakery beside the dungeon doors, I don't see the Lot again for eight years.

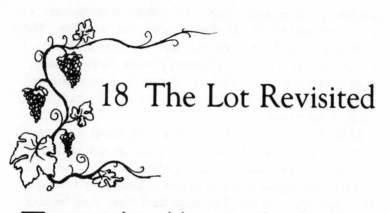

18 The Lot Revisited

THE RIVER is deep and the river is wide, milk and honey on the other side. Also on the other side, across the Pont Valentré, onward to the Boulevard Gambetta, are foie gras, prunes stuffed with purée of prunes, and Cahors wine. I am here for ten days, a little apprehensively, a tourist and a divorcé, renewing acquaintance. Will it be troubling, uncomfortable, being recognized and hailed in the market? Might it be better to be invisible, to hide in our empty flat and look down through a crack in the shutters? Each time I step outside there will be old familiar faces. I plunge ahead timorously, onto the streets. With me is the friend I live with on Long Island. She has never seen this corner of France and wants to.

No question, this is a bewitching town. The river Lot is mole-grey and lumbering, same as eight summers ago, and apart from some silting up here, eroding there, and changing course elsewhere, much the same, I suppose, as when Henry of Navarre led his army across it to capture the town. The countryside is unchanged except for the strip across the hills that has been lost to la déviation, the bypass. No serious loss, that scruffy ribbon of hillside, for motorists and behemoth trucks impatient to skip the town and hurtle on to Spain. The bypassing traffic is no loss at all to café society on the boulevard. The Palais tables are at traffic lights where lorries used to grind to a stop and pump petrol fumes in your face as you sipped your Pernod.

The approach to the Pont Valentré has flower beds. That's new. More flowers have appeared outside the Mairie and at roundabouts into and out of the town. The townsfolk are cross that a Parisian was imported to choose and organize these flowers. Any local gardener, they insist, would have done a far superior job.

To the left of Gambetta's statue is another advance in the cause of civic beautification, a lofty, thoroughly pleasant fountain with stone benches for people to sit on and sun themselves. Two smaller, plashy fountains with plants and benches have arrived beside the tourist office, and shade trees have been planted. So young and tiny are the shade trees that we shall be into the next millennium before they give enough shade to tempt anyone to sit here in the shrivelling sun. Never mind, effort has been made. Cahors is looking sprucer and more floral than ever before.

Wait. What is this monstrous arc of grey-and-maroon concrete columns behind the statue of burly Gambetta, son of Cahors, politician and patriot? An aesthetic statement? Does it serve a practical purpose? The answer we get at the tourist office is the French equivalent of 'Search me, mate'. One rumour is that the columns may be for hanging plants on, but they have apparently been there quite a while and no plants are hanging on them yet. Some philistine Cadurciens are as vexed by the fountains and columns as they are by the Parisian gardener. Here used to be parking space. Cars must now look for somewhere else, the very devil of a nuisance. Sylvette's opinion is that with the concrete columns behind him, Gambetta looks like Stalin. She tells us an attempt was made to clean him up, polish away the encrusted grime and pigeon droppings, but the cleansing chemicals made him look dirtier than before so the project was abandoned. She presents us with a jar of her mother's preserved goose.

Our bakery in the rue Nationale is here still, though rejigged, for no clear reason, so that when you enter you now turn left for your bread, not right. Behind the counter stands the same solemn, no-nonsense baker's wife. She recognizes me but we don't fall into each other's arms.

Ours was a business relationship, briskly civil, chat free. Same superlative bread. Oh my fur and whiskers! What to choose? I want it all.

At Prisunic's new improved food department I recognize several of the checkout women, and they me, but blinkingly, unsure when or who. The tobacconist's at the corner of the rue Nationale I avoid entering because the ebullient sprig who serves – he used to be a sprig, he is now a bearded husband and father – will cry out, 'Tiens, dis-donc, Monsieur Kenyon!' The only way to cut short the questions and answers would be to plead rusty French, but he would talk anyway, and what is the French for rusty? The hair of the handsome woman who serves in the newsagent's on the boulevard is a metallic argentine colour which is definitely not natural. I don't know what its natural colour is. Her hair has been every shade. A sienna red endured as long as any. When she reaches an age when her hair ought to be argentine it will be bronze, sable, or pumpkin. Bravo, Madame! Dyeing the hair is life-affirming and to be applauded.

The heat is such that for the first time ever I am buying bottled water, gallons of it: Evian, Contrex, Badoit, Vittel, Vichy, all different, some quite nasty, others good, one with laxative properties, so the label says, another stupendous for the liver. The flat in the rue Nationale has been rented to a French family I have never met, but this being August they are away and Victoria and I have moved in. Here is the piano we all intended to learn to play, forgotten kitchen china, dusty beams, my books in the study with the three doors. Since I am here I might as well have the books, the worthwhile ones, transported to Long Island. The slanting, fissured veranda supported by bent rods is still holding. All the same, I shall not be jumping up and down on it.

The despatching of the books turns out to be pretty gruelling. In retrospect I should have parcelled them up in cardboard boxes and taken them to the post office, but at the time it seemed simpler to hand the chore to the town's biggest removals firm and be done with it. The firm is efficient, as it should be considering the fee. They do not wish to go so far as to pack the books but they can give me a crate. When I have filled it and addressed and nailed down the lid they will collect it, ship it to Marseilles, and thence by cargo boat to New York. Who knows, perhaps aboard the *Atlantic Cognac*.

The finely-wrought, cubic yard of wooden crate weighs a ton. Two tons. I can't lift it but I can push and drag it. With help it goes into the car boot, the lid of which now gapes open, blanking out any view through the rear window. Taking a short cut to the rue Nationale along an invariably empty one-way alley, I am faced with a car heading the wrong way towards me. Being a French car it is not going to reculer, to back up. The driver is a chic young Frenchwoman, one of the weaker sex. They are the worst. Already she is honking her horn at me and flapping exasperated hands. 'Reculez, imbécile!' she mouths. She is not going to reverse and that is that. The French never reverse. Bearing down may be a steamroller, armed bandits, packs of rabid jackals, the French do not reverse. With no view of anything that might be behind, but beyond caring, I reverse along the alley and into a space. The chic woman accelerates past, chin in air, a scowl on her face.

Sumo wrestlers would need to be hired to bring the crate up to the flat, so I manhandle it inside the dungeon doors and bring the books down, a choice hundred or so. Encyclopaedias and atlases. All my old Thurber. Scrapbooks of clippings from newspaper reporting days, not that they have once been looked at or are likely to be. An ancient Byron (ah, him). *The Adventures of Fanny Hill*, furtively bought on my first or second trip to Paris and smuggled back through Dover years before London's pornography trials of the early sixties (Mervyn Griffith-Jones, prosecutor of *Lady Chatterley's Lover*: 'Would you allow your wife or your servant to read this book?'). Customs declarations have to be filled in, nails bought to fix the crate's lid, and for the address a hallucinogenic black marker pen. *Ensure ventilation in place of use.* By the time the crate is ready I have bloodied thumbs and sweat in my eyes. Curses I never knew I knew have echoed ringingly through the doors and along the rue Nationale. Only one bloke with a trolley arrives to heave the loaded crate into a truck so I am required to assist. Huff, puff, creak, crack. Six weeks later a New York removals firm, paid in advance, deposits the crate on the lawn. Perhaps some of these books are of sentimental value. They had better be.

We have rented a car and do tourist things: prehistoric caves, St Cirq-Lapopie, Albi with its Toulouse-Lautrec museum and a brick cathedral which looks more like a fortress than a house of God. We drive, goggle at fields of sunflowers, swallow chilled mineral water, and return to Cahors for supper chez Françoise, one evening, and with Elizabeth and Jean another. Jean has retired from driving rental cars from town to town. He and Elizabeth, MBE, are saving their pennies for a world tour.

Jim and Peggy Wolfe left the Lot for Tasmania, and Jim has died.

Jeff and Sally Stride are not here either. They are the guests of an Italian magnate in Tuscany. The magnate has promised to buy every painting they paint of his estate in a two-week period. My mind's eye sees Jeff and Sally painting a fresh painting every fifteen minutes in a frenzy of squeezed tubes and flying paint. Cash in the bank at last!

Remember cèpes (*boletus edulis*), the prized wild mushrooms priced in the market somewhere below truffles and foie gras, but not much below? We hear of trouble over cèpes. Outsiders with flashlights and rakes have been stealing into the beech and oak woods at night and making off with baskets of cèpes which the locals consider their private property. Violence has broken out and fines and prison sentences imposed. In the Corrèze, abutting the Lot's northern boundary, a farmer

202

in his deux-chevaux tried to run down a foreigner (from Angoulême). Another cèpe thief, a Turkish forestry worker, has been shot at. Perhaps the cèpe thieves should bring their baskets to Britain where cèpes, or penny buns, are left to moulder in the woods. The season is brief – September to the first frost – but the pickings should be worth their while. One family in the Corrèze reportedly makes 150,000 francs (£15,000 approximately) each autumn from gathering and selling cèpes, and tax free too, because who is going to declare it? *Larousse Gastronomique* has a dozen recipes for cèpes. Smothered cèpes, for example, where you simmer them in butter with a pinch of salt and a squirt of lemon. Nothing easier. In the Lot they are often eaten with confit, but I for one won't be gathering them. Most mushrooms look alike to me and some are deadly. *Larousse* shows photos of the deadly ones, nauseatingly describes the symptoms of mushroom poisoning, and aplogizes for introducing 'a rather terrifying picture in a work dedicated to gastronomy'. Italy, the world's biggest eater of fungus, imports cèpes from here in the south-west. Nutritionally they do not amount to much. Some Lotois say cèpes cure rheumatism but give you flu.

Polly arrives penniless, owing money to the taxi from the station. She is back from a holiday with friends in West Africa: Niger, Benin, Togo. Instead of money she has hair-raising stories of dysentery-inducing food and hitch-hiking in the wrong direction through deserts and mountains in vans low on petrol, filled with goats, driven by wild men with beards. She wants to return some day.

Polly guides us through the countryside to a restaurant at Goujounac (population 199) for Sunday lunch. We sit at a table on the terrace overlooking the deserted village square. Polly peruses the menu and says, 'Let's start with the foie gras.'

Attagirl, let's. We have kept abreast so know that no longer need we fear fatted goose and duck liver as the killer it was believed to be in the innocent seventies and eighties. The slogan for the nineties: Live Longer, Eat Foie Gras! The National Institute of Health and Medical Research in Lyon has found that the chemical composition of goose and duck fat is closer to olive oil (good) than to butter (bad). Foie gras contains saturated fat but does not dramatically increase cholesterol and may contain a fatty acid that has a positive effect on blood platelets, thereby improving cardiovascular health. So there.

Here in the south-west the diet is higher in saturated fat than anywhere in the industrialized world. Twice as much foie gras is eaten in the Lot and the neighbouring *département* of Gers than anywhere else in France, and fifty times as much as in the United States. I have no figure for the amount eaten in Britain but probably a middle road between France and America. The tricky part is that fewer people die of heart attacks in the south-west than elsewhere in France: 80 annually out of every 100,000 middle-aged men in the Toulouse area, compared with 145 for the rest of the country, and 315 in the United States. The rate of liver disease, on the other hand, is twice as high in France as in America.

So there are other factors, imponderables, and more research is needed, as when is it not? Onward, the march of science!

Polly tells us that the French linger less over their meals than they did ten years ago when I was here. As she is the only one of the family still living in France, and therefore au fait, I pay attention.

She says, 'They eat fewer courses and take less time over meals. Almost always now they eat the meat and veg together, not as separate courses. They'll even eat a sandwich for lunch, though they're not nearly as far along that road as Americans. They still want to sit and take at least an hour over lunch. They like two serious meals a day – not many bother with breakfast – but they're not fat because the food is balanced, the portions aren't huge, and they don't nibble on junk food and lug vast vats of popcorn into the cinema. The food industry is flourishing. The microwave is here and more and more prepared foods. We have innumerable brands of light food, and stores specializing in frozen food – frozen snails, frozen frog's legs, Chinese, everything.'

We brood on cheese. When our caravan came to rest in the Lot in the mid-seventies, industrial pasteurized cheesemaking on a grand scale (Caprice des Dieux, Frère Jacques, Fleur de l'Hermitage) was getting under way. Now it threatens to take over. O my serious farmhouse cheeses long ago! Pipsqueaks in Brussels want to make pasteurized milk compulsory for all cheese. Adieu, our Cantal and our Cabécou, not to mention Camembert, Brie, Saint-Marcellin and Saint-Nectaire (Appellation d'Origine Contrôlée). At a meeting of the Association France-Grande Bretagne in Paris, Prince Charles has raged – protested anyway – against the bureaucrats and their 'minimum hygiene standards'. My vote goes to Prince Charles. When did a wedge of Camembert kill anyone and what a way to go anyway. Who was it described Camembert as smelling like the feet of God? Off with their heads!

While griping, what about the *Marseillaise*? If *God Save the Queen* is morbid (Kate's word, not mine), the *Marseillaise*, in the opinion of a sizeable number of French, is downright bloodthirsty and should be given new words, i.e. pasteurized. The irrigating of ditches and furrows with the blood of the foe is deemed objectionable. What else should one do with foes? Kiss them? At least they don't seem bent on frigging about with the tune, or not yet. With any luck, both matters will by next week, and with proper regard to sanity, have been resolved, the *Marseillaise* and cheese. Pesky busybodies, a pox on them!

Polly says, 'You met a motorist who wouldn't back up? C'est normal.'

The chic madam's cheek in not backing up must have got under my skin. On the edge of Dartmoor, where my brother lives, the lanes are so serpentine and skinny that somebody has to back up, and unhesitatingly one or the other does, sometimes so promptly and Englishly as to be unaware, twisting round for a view of a sheep behind, that the opposing vehicle is doing likewise, retreating from sight round a twist in the leafy lane. Three minutes is about right for each to wait in a lay-by before venturing forward to discover what has happened to the other, whereupon both meet again.

'The further south you go the madder the driving,' says Polly, who has travelled more widely on the Continent than I have. 'The French think Italian drivers are the maddest – fast, macho, always sounding their horns. Italy has a campaign for the rights of fast-lane motorists. But it's the survival of the fittest in Paris too. Parisians are always trying to overtake as a matter of honour. The Germans have no speed limit on their motorways but they're disciplined and prudent. The French dismiss the British as crazy because we drive on the left but they'll admit we are reasonably safe. Portugal has five times as many car crashes as Britain.'

All this sounds fair. When Lucy took driving lessons in Cahors her instructor kept crying out, 'Plus vite! Plus vite!'

Polly says she has read that the Lot is the *département* with the biggest concentration of British, particularly over the last few years. 'They rushed in for second homes in the seventies, then it was calm, then another surge from 1988 which is still going on. Some of the Lotois dislike the British invasion. It's the same old thing, the foreigners coming in and paying house prices the natives aren't prepared to pay, though they'll sell for every penny they can get. They grumble that we don't bring in much money, we bring in our own Bovril and Bird's Custard, and there are too many of us. There's a fear among the Lotois that they will be swamped and lose their identity, or so the intellectuals say. I haven't noticed people going about looking frightened. Most of the French I know prefer the relaxed Spanish and Italian way of life to the British. They see us as unable to enjoy ourselves, hypocritical, and too stiff and polite. The old stereotypes. Then they meet one of us and are surprised if the stereotype doesn't fit.'

Madame is back for our orders. 'Bonjour, Madame. Oui, il fait beau. Oui, nous avons décidé. On commence avec le foie gras . . .'

Epilogue

W HAT KEEPS me on the east end of Long Island where I mulishly resist acquiring a word processor, teach occasionally, and do my best to make a joyful noise in the choral society? 'You must take responsibility!' pleads our charismatic conductor. 'Your entrances! Your cut-offs! The dynamics!' August, September, hurricanes carry off houses into the ocean and topple trees. Should the immense Norwegian maple in our back garden topple, that will be the end of either the house or the garage, depending which way the maple goes.

Her name is Victoria, a native of the exotic Bronx – to me the Bronx is wrenchingly exotic – freelance book designer, writer of jokebooks (*Westward Ho Ho Ho!* Viking, 1992), and if required, speaker of inventive French with correct gesturing. She is capable of jokes in French (What did Edith Piaf sing while tossing the salad? *Je ne vinaigrette rien*) but will desist if asked. She sings too. Henry IV found Paris well worth a mass. I find Victoria well worth the hurricanes.

Speaking of songs, Rossini – *Largo al factotum della città – largo!* – born two hundred years ago, would have been at home in the Lot. Tournedos Rossini? That is where you sauté a filet mignon in butter, plump it on croûtons fried in butter, then park on top foie gras and truffles heated and tossed in guess what. Over this, Madeira sauce made from the pan juices. Rossini would fill a silver syringe with a paste of foie gras and truffles which he then discharged

207

into cooked macaroni. His maladies included gallstones, urinary infections, depression, neurasthenia, and chronic indigestion. Still, he lived to be seventy-six.

Catherine teaches in London. She lives with a man I have not met, an Englishman my age, in bosky Highgate, and has bought herself a Peugeot. She has visited us on Long Island but it is to France she returns when the opportunity arises. (Gustave has passed from the scene.) Matters were so managed last summer that she and the girls were together in Cahors. Only for two weeks in the case of Lucy and Kate because they have moved across the Atlantic and two measly weeks per annum is all the American workplace allows.

Lucy took a degree in French and philosophy at London University, went into publishing, and now lives and works in Manhattan. This time round she is legal. She won her green card in a lottery.

Kate worked for three years in reception at the Hôtel Regina, opposite the Louvre, and as a housekeeper at the Georges V, off the Champs Elysées. The message she kept receiving was that as a woman she would never advance far in the French hotel industry, a point that her hotel school did not come up with. She lives in Brooklyn, and works on Wall Street at the international trading desk of a French bank (not the Crédit Agricole). So much for hotel school.

No worry about Kate's legality on these shores. She is Kate the Yank, born in Illinois. Through Kate I received my green card.

Polly's degree from the University of Montpellier is in audio-visuel, meaning radio, TV, and movies, with art history and German thrown in. She au-paired in Hamburg for a year. She was not arrested before she started as was one au-pair we know, but she was put out in the snow with her suitcase at five minutes notice for answering back to the Hausfrau. She is in Paris translating TV scripts at top speed for a Franco-Canadian co-production of a cops-and-robbers series with Christopher Plummer titled *Counterstrike*, or in

French, *Force de Frappe*. She would make a useful technical adviser on foie gras.

The three girls were with Victoria and me on Long Island for Christmas.

Polly said, 'The unit manager took me to lunch and we had sautéed foie gras, pinkish inside, you could see sort of veins and jelly stuff. The unit manager is from Béarn in the Pyrenees and he said sautéed foie gras was a glory of the south-west. I'd never heard of it. I've never had foie gras any way but cold and dense. I asked the waitress to take it back and cook it some more. She refused. She said it was supposed to be moist and if it was cooked more it would become rubbery. The unit manager agreed, they ganged up on me, so I ate it as it was. Delicious! It was très fin, very delicate. We had it with two or three little cut up carrots. Bread, of course. I asked my friend Domie about sautéed foie gras. She's one hundred per cent from the south-west – the Lot. She'd never heard of it sautéed either.'

I am fond and foolish enough to want to know from the girls such silliness as how their French compares. 'Polly's is fastest,' Lucy and Kate answer in unison, and fall about laughing. French or English, Polly tends to speak at the rate of a machine gun. Or she did. At twenty-four or thereabouts she may be slowing down.

Her sisters say Polly passes as French. Polly denies this. The French suspect she is not French but are unable to place her, she says. One reason she is so pleased to be with us on Long Island for Christmas is that we are all speaking English. In France she never speaks English. She worries she might lose it.

Lucy has not thought or dreamed in French since she left France ten years ago. Kate speaks French at work every day. She sometimes still thinks in French, and when she talks with her sisters she will often switch to French. She says she makes the same gender mistakes – le instead of la, la instead of le – she was making fifteen years ago. Parisians have told Lucy her accent combines English and the Midi.

'A very drunk man once told me I was from Montélimar,' she says. 'I don't know where Montélimar is, only that they make nougat there.'

I remind them sternly who it was started them off in French with lists of vocabulary and *Frère Jacques* at the holiday house in Catus and at the kitchen table in the rue Joffre.

'Oui, Papa,' they say.